Kingdom of the Wolf

Book 1

A Lunar Courtship

By Robier Mordecai

For my friends and family, thank you for believing in me!

"Even a man who is pure of heart,

And says his prayers by night

May become a wolf

When the wolf bane blooms and the autumn moon is bright."

Chapter 1

The moon was high in the dark and foreboding sky, clouds were rolling in front of the bright full orb. The sudden loss of light made the forest seem darker than it was. Though for Dean this made no difference, he could still see as well as in the daylight. He looked around the forest, his eyes scanned through the darkness. Lifting his snout and testing the air, rooting out his prey. His mind was filled with the wonders of the night, throbbing and quivering with the possibilities. He caught the whiff of a small animal; he took in another nostril full of the cold night air, burning the inside of his nose and lungs. It was a rabbit, not a banquet by any means, but a nice snack none the less. He was off, the sudden noise he made scared the rabbit, which in a state of panic darted off. The chase was on, he had hunted in this forest for a long time, this was his playground, and the rabbit would not get away.

Dean was a werewolf; a child of the moon and with her beckoning call will become a wolf and hunt. He was bitten seven years ago when he was only nineteen. He had snuck out of his parent's house and was partying with some friends in the forest near his home. But unbeknown to them there was a pack of fully turned werewolves in that area. These were not the same as Dean; they no longer had their human minds. They did not see people as Dean and the rest of the werewolf community does, only food. They attacked, most of his friends were killed and though wounded he survived all be it a little different. His wounds were grave indeed, his left arm shredded to bits, his left eye and cheek were ripped from his head. Also a chunk was missing from his hip exposing the bone and joint. He was close to oblivion when someone found him and contacted the emergency services. His wounds were so extensive no one could believe he had survived for as long as he had. The paramedics had never seen anything like it, there were body parts and entrails scattered throughout the clearing. Also there was so much blood it had soaked into the ground, turning the area into a quagmire of repugnant gore. Most stared blankly at the carnage, while some lost the contents of their stomachs. He was awake for all of this, but he felt no pain after a while. At the time he thought it was the adrenaline that was pumping through his veins, but now he knew it was the werewolf venom getting to work. The thing that stuck in his mind though was the smell, he smelt things humans barely perceived that night and every night since.

He was ducking and weaving, under and between trees and exposed roots. His muscles began to tire, his heart was pounding in his chest and his breath was becoming ragged. But he was also catching up with the poor unfortunate animal. The rabbit dove to the right, trying to evade him. It would have worked, had Dean not been gifted with reflex's greater than any normal wolf. He saw his chance; he pounced, while in mid-air he saw the rabbit rustling through the undergrowth. He was going to be on target, his heightened senses hadn't failed him, and they never had. He landed on the small animal with his front paws, instantly breaking the creatures back. He had been perfecting that move for many years now, though he had never got used to the loud crack made by the animal's spine breaking under his weight. He took the small carcass into his jaws and bounded off into the darkened forest, he could feel dawn drawing near.

The next thing he can remember was waking up in a bed of ferns. He blinked out the sleep that still nagged at the back of his eyes, rubbing his face he felt the new stubble that had already begun to grow there. He opened his mouth and yawned loudly, his fang like canines receding back into his upper jaw. He always felt well rested after his nocturnal antics. He knew he would be as naked as the day he was born and he knew there would be blood covering his face. There always was. Lifting his nose to the light whipping air. There was water nearby; at least he could wash the blood off his face before anyone saw him. It would be difficult to explain why he was totally butt naked and covered in blood.

He stood and stretched out his body, ridding the weariness from his joints and muscles, moaning loudly with waking pleasure. Running his fingers through his bright golden hair he pulled out bits off leaves and broken twigs. Dried sludge covered his hands and feet. He always looked a mess when he awoke from his slumber in nature. He scratched at an itch on his stomach and followed down and scratched at his pubic hair. He felt something and pulled at it, whatever it was, it was stuck fast with his curly blonde hair. He looked down and couldn't see anything, only dried blood. He took a firmer hold on the object, gritted his teeth and pulled. It came away with more than a few of his hairs. He whimpered in pain, he felt around the area where the thing had been, no there was no bald patch there thank God he thought. He took a look at the object.

"Ewwww," came involuntary from his lips.

It was the small skull of the unfortunate rabbit from last night, stuck in his pubic hairs with its own blood. He must have fallen asleep on the body off the small rabbit last night. That was the only problem with this gift (or curse depending on the way you look at it) you can't be a little squeamish. He threw the offending object away and shuddered at the thought of being laid on a corpse. He sniffed again and followed the scent of water; He had to get rid of this blood before anyone saw him, once he had to run because the people thought he was a murderer or something, if only they knew the truth he thought. It would be pitchforks, torches and anything silver he thought smiling. They were small people with small minds. Werewolves aren't like they are in the movies; they still retain their intelligence and sense of morality. Only fully turned werewolves lost that, nothing more than larger and stronger wolves. However they were far more dangerous to both humans and werewolves. They didn't care whether they smelt like kin or not, if they weren't part of the pack they were nothing but food.

He came out into a clearing surrounded by trees and bushes; he sniffed the air cautiously and could sense no danger. Looking up he judged it was around five in the morning by the position and brightness of the sun, he knew he wouldn't bump into anyone this deep in the forest. He walked over to the edge of the small lake that was in the middle of the clearing. Crouching on all fours he tensed the muscles in his legs, forcing all the strength into his thighs he pushed himself from the ground. Propelling himself nine feet into the air, diving into the lake with minimal splashing. The momentum forcing him so far below the surface he could reach out and touch the lakebed, looking around with his augmented eyes he saw small fish darting from him and the plants swaying in the current his dive had caused. Glancing at the surface he saw the fragmented shafts of light penetrating through the rippling water as though he were trapped within a beautiful blue-green sapphire. With a werewolf's gift the world took on a whole other facet of splendour, they could see beyond the mundane and into the very soul of the earth. They could see the grace in the swaying grass, the serenity of a passing cloud, the majesty of the full moon and the mystery of a vast, dark forest. This was a gift and should never be considered a curse.

He kicked off the lakebed feeling the soft fine sand between his spread bare toes and headed for the surface, breaking the serene stillness above. Splashing through the cool, refreshing water. Enjoying the freedom isolation granted. He could be his real self here; he could be Dean the werewolf. In this place he didn't need the wall he had built to shield himself from everyone. His web of lies and misdirection wasn't needed here, in this, his natural habitat. He raced to the shore as swiftly as his werewolf altered muscles would allow. When he had reached the shore he scrambled out of the water on all fours, shaking droplets of water from his smooth, soft skin. Growling he ran at a large redwood tree, extending his wolfen claws he jumped at the vast trunk. Digging his claws into the bark, chunks of it flew through the air as he raced vertically up the massive tree. As he reached as far as his bulk would allow he loosed a drawn out, piercing howl, birds squawked in panic and fled from the nearby trees. Animals called out in either response or fear throughout the awakening forest. His heart was beating madly in his chest. He had to get rid of all this excess energy before he headed for home. Jumping from the tree he dropped thirty-five feet to the ground below, landing with nothing more than a low thud. He rose to his feet slowly as his claws retreated back into their hidden sheaths underneath his human nails. Looking down he could see that his penis was fully engorged and erect, its bulbous purple-pink head revealing itself from within its foreskin. One downside of the werewolf genes was an unquenchable libido. He knew he would have to reach a climax; it was the only way to rid himself of his erection.

Finding a small outcropping jutting over the lake, he sat himself down with his legs hanging over the edge, the tips of his toes skimming the surface of the cool water. Lying back onto the soft dew coated grass, his bare chest raising rhythmically, his nipples hardening from the cool dawn air and his own desires. Running his hands over the tender nodules of flesh, giving one a playful nip. He moaned quietly, hardly perceivable as the sharp sting turned to ripples of pleasure. He could smell his own musk; it stank of pheromones laden with his unbridled sexual appetite. Letting his hands wander, he left his nipple behind, caressing his lithe and smooth though deceptively firm chest. He let his hand move lower down his body, stroking the undulations and ripples of his lightly

8

muscled and likewise smooth abdomen. Skirting his genitalia, his hard member twitching in perceived anticipation, he stroked his hairless inner thighs. His body hadn't changed much since he was bitten as werewolves age much slower than humans, so he still appeared in the final grasp of puberty. Retaining his boy like looks and young, fertile body. He played with his pubic hairs, curling them round his finger, pulling on them gently. His hand moved lower, tickling his scrotum, cupping his testicles in his hand he squeezed them lightly. Rolling them within their sac, his moaning grew louder. Moving his hand up and onto his penis, rubbing the bulbous head now fully exposed. He moved his hand down to the hilt and traced the long blue-purple vein all the way to the top. Running his index finger along the slit, the digit glistened with pre-come. Licking it he tasted his own juices, his taste buds recognizing the familiar salty tang. He took a gentle grip of his cock, pulling back on the foreskin, pulling it back as far as it would go. His eyes closing as his speed and pleasure increased. Knowing it wouldn't take him long he slowed his pace and took a tighter grip, he wanted to savour it for as long as he could. Pulling back on his foreskin, letting it linger on the ridge of his glands, before pushing it up and over its head. He was concentrating all his attention on the very tip of his penis, which released a constant stream of lubricating pre-come in appreciation. He wanted to continue but his animal like instinct that still lingered at the back of his mind urged him to speed up. Though he tried to resist, even when he knew it was pointless. He started to wank faster and faster, his body squirming with sexual pleasure. Then along came the recognizable pressure deep in the pit of his stomach, then the undeniable pleasure of release. His eyes shot open as his testicles tightened. His penis' head spasm as a vast amount of semen erupted from the slit. It splashed on his chest and stomach, a string of it connecting his bell end with his stomach. Great globules of it covered his pubic hair. His body shuddered as the pleasure shot through him. He just laid there breathing heavily, his mind reeling from the climax. Time for another bath he thought to himself and dragged his energy sapped body from the soft and comfortable grass. His penis became flaccid but still dripped semen.

He took a step off the outcrop and dropped into the water below, cleaned the mess off his body and pulled himself out and back onto the bank. Now it was time for the worst part of the lunar cycle, finding his damned clothes. He lifted his nose to the air, trying to catch a scent that has become as familiar as his own. His mind filled with the scents of the forest, but where was that particular one. He caught the slight hint of the strong smelling exotic herbs he tied to his clothes every lunar cycle. He had learnt that trick years ago and it had never failed him. Before journeying off to follow the scent, he stood a while to allow the bright morning sun to warm his smooth body and young skin.

He came to a part that was familiar to him, he remembered this was the place the change had begun to come over him. Looking around he saw the plastic bag poking out from under a log. Sitting on the log he began to lay out his clothes from last night. Three more days of freedom, then he would again have to become something he wasn't. For one month at least, the lunar cycle would begin anew and he would once again be free. But for only three days, he thought to himself as he was pulling on his kaki coloured combat trousers. He eased himself into a tight black t-shirt before topping his look with an open white shirt. A yawn overtook him and he stretched out his spine which protested with pops and cracks. When he slept in a funny position he would always end up with an ache or creak. He would have to organise his sleeping arrangements more carefully next time he thought to himself. Taking out a small pocket mirror from the bag he looked at himself in it, ruffling his hair and wiping sleep out of his eyes. Presentable enough he thought as he stuffed the mirror into one of his many combat pockets. He took out a shoulder bag from the other bag and put everything else in it. He slung it over his shoulder and started to head towards the many trekking routes that criss-cross the forest. If anyone saw him now they would just think he was another walker, a perfect disguise. A pleasant smile, a small nod or an occasional 'hello, how are you' and no one gave you a second thought.

He came into view of the small town where he lived; it was nestled in a valley with an incredibly vast forest all around it. A perfect habitat for a werewolf. The town was called Redbridge, due to the red cliffs further down the valley, just a few miles from the town itself. There were no other werewolves around here; it was very rare for one to see another of their kind. It was forbidden to have lasting relations within the human world, just in case they were found out. Only those who lived in the werewolf towns and enclaves were allowed to live together. However there were unconfirmed rumours of some werewolves breaking the rules and living together, But they were in love, love being the only thing powerful enough to force them to ignore the code. He stood on the red cliffs, looking to see if anyone was around. Seeing he was alone he leapt from the cliffs edge. He landed on a boulder halfway up; he loved testing his abilities to their limits. He jumped the rest of the way and landed on an old jeep trail that was seldom used.

He walked the few miles into town, keeping his head down and trying not to attract any attention. That was the most dangerous thing to a werewolf, attention, if you get too complacent, you made too many slip ups then people would get suspicious, then it was game over. Oh they wouldn't know the truth, but they would keep an eye on you, which would make it difficult for you to disappear each month. Keep your head down; make acquaintances not friends, leave no trail. This was the code all werewolves followed; it was just easier that way. If it got too hot, you're gone, no trail, no one to wonder where you are, no problems. Dean had seen what can happen when you don't follow the code and it had left a scar on his very soul. He could never be forgiven for what happened. It was lonely this is true, but werewolves felt freedom no human could ever claim to feel. It was a gift but a gift with downsides.

He opened the door that led to his apartment building and went in. Entering the lobby of his apartment building he slowly climbed the stairs to the third floor, his leg muscles complaining after the nights overuse. He scrambled around in his pocket for his key as he came to his door. He opened it and walked in.

"Dean, where have you been this early in the morning?" a familiar voice came from behind him.

He turned to see that his next door neighbour was stood at her door, her dark chestnut hair falling in curls around her face. Darkly inquisitive, feline eyes stared at his through strands of red curls, twinkling at the anticipation of a piece of gossip. She was by far the most nosey person he had ever known.

"Nowhere special, just for a walk in the woods," said Dean.

"You do that very often Dean, surely there can't be that much for you to see," said the woman.

"Well I have a secret Val," he revealed.

"Ooh really do tell, it will go no further, I promise," Val becoming excited.

He smiled wickedly inside as he thought about his cheeky plan. He knew he shouldn't really treat someone like this even if they did ask for it by being so nosey. But he couldn't help himself.

"Well the thing is, I'm...............a.................twitcher," drawing out his explanation with relish.

"You twitch so you go to the woods?" her tone turning confused.

Dean couldn't believe how dense she was, he thought it was an act, but obviously it wasn't.

"No, I'm a bird watcher, I study birds, that's why I spend so much time in the woods," a well-rehearsed lie slipped easily from his lips.

"Oh," she said.

"I have to go Val, I have work in a bit," he said quickly, cutting her off before she could tardy him anymore.

"Oh ok," she said and left.

Dean closed the door and shook his head. She really angered Dean, with her constant questioning. He just wanted to be left alone in his solitude. He had lied, he didn't have work at all, and he always took the lunar cycle off. It was just easier that way; at least he didn't have to explain why he was eating raw meat. For some reason werewolves had cravings for raw flesh even when in human form, but it was just one of them downsides. He sat down on his couch and switched on the TV. He thought he would watch some pointless daytime TV and then have a sleep before the next change that night. As the lunar cycle was three days long and a werewolf changes each night, it was exhausting. He watched a mind-numbing and disturbing chat show which featured a young man graphically explaining the joy of his love life with his girlfriend who was sixty years his senior. Who just happened to be his long lost paternal grandmother. After an hour he could feel his eyelids to droop and he knew it was time for him to retire. He sluggishly removed his clothes and slipped into the fresh cool bed. There beneath the covers he began to feel strange, as though there was someone near. Someone watching him. He had felt it before when he was with his mentor, the man who taught him to control his gift, to use it to his advantage. It was the way his kind communicated at distance, like an almost empathic link. They aren't able to actually speak to one another but they can transmit feelings. Both physical and emotional. He could feel someone's hands resting on his bare hips, slowly moving up his body caressing his chest. The hands moved further up till they came to rest on his shoulders, he could almost feel the hot sticky breath on his lips as the phantom mouth moved in for a kiss. Then it was gone. The empathic link was broken somehow. He rolled over and tried to think if he had sensed any others around this morning. There were dead animals apart from the rabbit, no smells, nothing, he was alone here. As far as he knew, there were no other werewolves in the area. After a few hours tossing and turning his eyes grew heavy and closed, he dropped off into a fitful, disturbed slumber.

He awoke later that night around nine pm. He felt the usual aching and tightness in his joints, signalling the change was starting. It was over two whole hours early, it shouldn't be starting now. He began to panic. He swung out of bed, opened the wardrobe and threw on some clothes. He didn't have the time to worry about appearance; it would not be long till the change was upon him. If he was to change in the middle of town then it would be goodbye myth, hello reality. That was not acceptable. He threw open his door slammed it shut and ran down the stairs two at a time. He didn't have long, he would have to be quick, that meant being reckless a very dangerous thing to be for a werewolf. He came out of his apartment block and turned to the left and down the back of his building. He threw his bag over his shoulder and extended his claws. Seeing his reflection in one of the ground floor windows, he saw his eyes had turned a shade of blue so bright and deep they looked utterly unnatural on a human face. He jumped, dug into the wall with his claws and crawled up the vertical surface. He reached the top and landed on all fours, where he involuntarily let out a long drawn mournful howl. He clamped his mouth shut, feeling the oversized canines growing longer. Shit he thought to himself, this was going to be close. He ran to the other side of the building and raced full pelt towards the forest. As he drew close to the edge he pushed all his strength into his legs and jumped. He landed perfectly on the roof off the other building opposite; he took another run and jumped towards the forest. He just made it to the forest edge, but he landed awkwardly badly twisting his ankle. It did not matter now as the adrenaline coursing through his veins was blocking out the pain. But he knew come morning it would be agonizingly painful. He ran as far into the darkening forest as he could before the change took over. Then the pain came, it was like being torn apart and crushed all at the same time. He fell to the floor and ripped at his clothes, tearing them from his body. He stood on all fours and tried to relax his muscles, he knew it wouldn't work, his change was in overdrive but he had to try. The pain grew; his muscles began cramping all over the place. This was also one of the downsides.

His stomach was being pulled in as his internal organs began rearranging themselves. His ribs fractured in places and repositioned themselves. His pelvis was being forced further up, causing his spine to arch. His feet began to elongate, claws slipping from his toes. His skull started to elongate as well creating a small snout. Thankfully this was where he always blacked out due to the excruciating pain.

Chapter 2

He awoke in his form of a wolf. As he rose he closed his eyes and inhaled the smell of this place. A shiver of familiarity started in his paws, worked its way through his entire body and made his heart miss a beat. He was home. His dull blonde fur coat was long and shaggy, hanging low on his stomach. His deep blue, luminous eyes stood out against his golden appearance. Stretching out his body with his paws out front he swished his long fox like tail. Curling his body he licked at his underbelly. He rolled around on the forest floor covering himself in dirt and getting brown leaves stuck in his fur. Just like any dog he enjoyed getting filthy. He looked up at the moon, the perfect circular shape easing Dean's tension, lightening his mood. As the true full moon always did. He loped off into the deep darkness. He was just running tonight he thought to himself, just having fun, not hunting, nothing but fun. He ran around the forest, enjoying himself. Loving it when animals ran from him, but they had nothing to fear not tonight. He ran up to a cliff whose sheer sides led to a river below. He stood on the edge, lowered his head breathing heavily. His head shot up and his vocal cords issued a howl of pure and unadulterated joy. Before following up with another, this one longer and louder. That'll shit up the people in town he thought to himself. He heard a noise behind him and his ears pricked up instantly. Something was stalking him he realised. He slowly walked along the edge, quickly darting into the foliage. Now it was time for the hunted to become the hunter. He wasn't planning on hunting anything, but it was better being the predator than the prey.

He held his body low to the ground as he heard the soft padding of paws somewhere to the left of him. He rose from his hiding place silently, downwind so the other didn't know he was there. It had obviously lost him; maybe it was time for it to find him. He jumped out and landed behind the creature, now it had its back to the cliffs edge, instead of the other way round. He issued a low and menacing growl which reverberated in his chest cavity. It was a warning growl. The creature turned out to be a wolf, larger than Dean, it stopped dead when it heard the warning. Turning to face Dean, it held its ear low. Dean tested the air. Its scent betrayed it to be a fellow werewolf, he realised this must have been who had subconsciously communicated earlier that night. Now he understood why his change had come on so early, his wolf spirit had sensed this other and grew excited.

16

This werewolf was blacker than the deepest, darkest, starless and moonless night. But throughout his dark countenance there were light, almost silver strands of fur. When Dean's mind grasped the significance of this his heart skipped a beat in terror. Grey hair didn't mean the same as it did to mankind. Though it portrayed age as it does with humans, as a werewolf ages, they grow more powerful. This werewolf was old, very old. He had to handle this situation with extreme care, as one false move could spell his end. Sniffing at the soft night air he caught the scent of strong must, the air was full of testosterone. It was another male, which increased the inherent danger this being posed. But he could get nothing more from his scent. The other werewolf took a step towards Dean, who immediately took a step back and gave out another growl. Not through fear, even though he was petrified, but as part of his natural defensive mechanism. He had to appear strong, but even he knew that he was exuding the scent of fear in every droplet of sweat that came from his pores. The other wolf just sat down on its haunches, its tongue lolling from its jowls. It looked like it had come in peace, but Dean wasn't taking any chances. He circled the animal cautiously, looking for any sign of danger. His eyes were fixed so intently on the other werewolf he did not notice the cliffs edge, but the other did. The other werewolf jumped with a start and bounded towards Dean, who backed off slightly, but as he did his rear paws fell off the edge of the cliff. He began to fall, he pushed his paws into the ground for some purchase, but not having any fingers did have some drawbacks. He slipped over the edge, he closed his eyes, and not even a werewolf could survive that sort of fall. He felt a sharp pain in his right front leg, and then there was pressure. He opened his eyes and saw the other werewolf holding his leg in his mouth. He pulled Dean up and back over the cliffs edge. When he was safely away from danger the other wolf released him. He laid down next to Dean and began licking at the wound. Dean knew he was apologizing for hurting him. Dean stood and tested his leg, tentatively putting some weight on it, it was not bad. He looked at the other who was eyeing him concerned. Dean went over to the other werewolf and nuzzled the other with his snout at the base of his neck in way of thanks. This did not seem unwelcome and he reciprocated. Then Dean remembered the communication, he wanted to mate. He gave the other a sly look, licked the other's nose and ran off. He stopped at the tree line turned and looked at the other and cocked his head. If he wanted me he had to catch me first he thought to himself. He swished his tail provocatively as he walked into the forest. The other was obviously giving him a head start, because after a while, he gave out a low rumble of a coming ready or not and raced into the forest.

Dean was not going to make it easy; he was worth a little run at least. He ran through bushes, thorns snagging at his fur and flesh. He ducked under a fallen log, held up off the ground by a boulder. It was nice to be the chased instead of the chaser for once he thought. He heard the tell-tale rustling behind him. I'm not that easy he thought to himself. He dipped to the left sharply, skidding on some mud losing his momentum slightly. He ran at full pelt towards a tree, turning sharply as he got to it, sprung on his legs and twisted his midriff. He released some urine that splashed on the trunk of the tree, landing back on all fours gracefully and carried on running. Marking with his urine along the path, hoping that would confuse him enough. He stopped and doubled back; he got about a quarter of the way and dropped off to his right into the bushes. His urine was so full of pheromones he would not smell him here.

He saw a flash of pitch black fur go past. It had worked; he heard the other stop as the scent lessened. This was his chance. He broke from cover and ran in the opposite direction. The crashing alerted the other to his position. He was enjoying this. He heard the other running after him, he weaved and turned suddenly. But he could not lose him. He decided to give in. He slowed his pace very slightly and turned to run up a hill. He burst through some bushes and was confronted with the most beautiful view in the whole forest. It looked out on a vast lake, the moons bright light playing off its surface as the slight breeze caused ripples. The moon looked so large up here, almost like he could reach out and touch it. He was panting loudly; he hadn't run so much for a long time. He heard a low whimper and turned around to see the other walking slowly through the bushes, his tongue hanging panting even louder. He had run enough Dean thought to himself, he deserves his spoils. The other walked over and looked out on the lake, admiring the view. Dean walked over and rubbed his entire body along the others. He got to the head and nuzzled him, licking at his face.

The other werewolf turned and his vivid green eyes bore straight into Dean's soul, but somewhere beneath there was a longing, even fear. The eyes were glistening, almost like he was crying. But Dean knew that was impossible as in wolf form they couldn't cry, he had found that out first hand.

The other, grabbed Dean by his fur and tugged him down to the ground with care. He stood over him and nipped at Dean's ear, it stung slightly. Dean snapped back, not in anger but playfully. The other pulled back, looking at him prostrate on his back between his paws. He whined and prodded his neck with his nose. Telling him how lonely he was. Ah you want to be on top Dean thought, well that's one thing I'm not letting go without a fight. He knew he would lose, but he had to at least not look too eager. Dean grabbed the others foreleg in his jaws and yanked him off balance. As the other fell Dean leapt atop him. They both rolled around in the thick undergrowth, each vying and fighting for the top position. When they stopped rolling the other was on top of Dean. Just as the other was about to pin him, Dean pushed him away with his paws and leapt free. The other got up and stalked towards Dean. They circled one another, each eyeing the other with both lust and caution. The others tail gently stroked against Deans side, its long soft hair like a lovers caressing hand. The other werewolf drew closer and rubbed his flank against Deans. As they circled the next round the forest was filled with their scents, the scent of lust. The other werewolf buried his nose against Dean's neck. Dean could feel the others hot breath against his skin causing his heart to beat stronger and stronger as the other inhaled his scent. The other grabbed Dean by the scruff of the neck and pushed him to the floor. He gave out a yip of triumph.

He won thought Dean. He was laid on his side, looking up at the other with his ears bolt upright in excitement, his tail wagging furiously. He wanted it as much as the other; he just put on a bit of a show. Some foreplay for his pursuers benefit. The other moved closer towards Dean his head held low, he sniffed at Dean's stomach. Dean whimpered like an impatient pup, waiting to suckle. He was tormenting him he thought. The other looked at Dean with a mischievous look. He was and he knew it was excruciating, he thought to himself. He licked at Dean's nose, licking along the snout and nibbling his ears. Dean's leg was trembling with pleasure. Dean growled in impatience, the others teeth bared in reprimand, he had won after all. Dean just decided to go with the flow. He returned to licking and nuzzling Dean's neck. He moved further down his body, he skirted around his genitals with his tongue. Dean wriggled his hips; he wanted more attention than that. The other saw what he was doing and nipped his rear leg. Dean yelped in pain and surprise. Ow he thought to himself. The other moved to his tail and gently tugged at it with his teeth. Oh God this guy knows how to treat a wolf he thought to himself, his mind drifting with the pleasure. He couldn't focus on anything, his eyes blurred and all he could hear was his own whimpering. The other was licking at his rectum, teasing it with his tongue. He could feel his penis begin to become engorged with blood, its tip pushing its way out his tight fur sheath. The other was too content on playing with his anus to notice and Dean didn't want him to stop anyway. His leg was trembling faster and faster now. Pleasure coursing through his body, he had never felt anything like this before.

The other stopped and started to nibble at his tail again; he grabbed Dean's rear leg in his jaws and gently rolled him onto his back. He stuck his nose into Dean's genitals, licking away at his emerging penis and fur covered testicles, nibbling at the sensitive flesh that lay beneath. Dean let out an almost human like moan; this was what he had wanted. The feeling was amazing, the musty smell rising from both their hot bodies, flooding Dean's senses, setting his mind on fire. All else was shut out, it was just the two of them in the forest tonight. Dean closed his eyes and laid back; enjoying the intense attention the other was now paying to his balls and penis. His moaning grew deeper. Then the sensation stopped suddenly. Dean opened his eyes and saw the other standing over him, staring straight into his eyes. He knew what he wanted; he didn't have to be able to talk to convey his intentions. Dean rolled over onto his belly and raised his rear end. Lifting his tail to reveal the tight pinkish mound of his anus in amongst the soft, downy hair, he knew what was coming and feared it as much as he wanted it. He had never had intercourse as a wolf before, as a human yes but never as a wolf. The other went around to Dean's rear and sniffed at his anus. The others warm breath on it was almost unbearable, Dean nearly collapsed with the pleasure that ran through him. The other positioned himself behind Dean and mounted him. He gripped on to Dean's body by biting into his neck. The pain was soon driven away by the pleasure as the other started to enter Dean's anus. Soon the head was in and Dean began moaning again, his body writhing underneath the other. Dean pushed his hips backwards, he wanted all of him. That was all the signal the other needed and he pushed home. The other started to pull back a little. Dean moaned as he withdrew and then moaned louder as the fullness returned. The other sped up, thrusting in and out faster and faster. Dean bucked hard with pleasure threatening to throw the other off. He had to grip harder on to Dean's skin with his teeth, a canine popping through the surface. To Dean the pain perversely made the pleasure even more intense, his eyes closed, his teeth bared and growling loudly. He could feel the other speed up, their hips slapping together. The thrusts became shallower and more controlled as the canine like knot at the base of the others penis began to swell. Dean realised that if the knot should accidentally slip into him they would be 'tied' together for hours. But it soon became apparent this werewolf had many years' worth of experience behind him. The knot had now become fully dilated and roughly stretched the very opening of Dean's anus with each and every thrust, causing more and more pleasure for the both of them. Then suddenly he felt the hard, warm rod quiver and twitch against his muscles. The other held himself rigid within Dean. Seconds later warm, sticky semen coated the inside of Dean anal cavity. As this sexy old werewolf emptied each and every drop from his sizable reservoir in what seemed to be a never ending series of spurts. The other let out a howl so loud it nearly deafened Dean as he was brought to a climax. The other withdrew and sat down, panting heavy. Dean dropped to the floor his body sapped off every drop of energy by the pleasure. He rolled over to sleep when he felt the other nuzzling at his leg.

Dean looked at him, his eyes showing confusion. If he thought that I had any energy to do it again or do it to him he had another thing coming he thought to himself. The other hooked his nose under Dean's leg and rolled him on to his back again. He stuck a nose towards Deans genitals, Dean yipped in excitement. He wants to bring me off now he thought as the other began to lick at his penis. He tugged at the skin of Dean's sheath with his teeth, licking at his balls. Dean knew it would not take a lot. There was pre come already being ejected by his penis under the constant attention. Dean moaned as he felt his penis begin to spew semen, his testicles were emptying themselves completely. He looked to see the other lapping at the substance as it was released. The other licked every last drop up like a hungry puppy, cleaning Dean's penis of any remnants. With that done the other dropped down next to Dean

21

equally exhausted now. Dean rolled over and snuggled up to him, feeling his heat radiate from his body even through his thick coat. The soft snoring from the other lulled Dean to sleep. Just before he dropped off he thought just how content and comfortable he felt.

Chapter 3

He awoke the next morning, a little after dawn. He stretched out his body, the joints popping and cramp being driven from his muscles. He looked over to see if the other he had stayed with was awake yet. He was gone, there was no one there. He was alone again. He stood and looked around, there was wolf prints leaving off into the forest. He left during the night. He growled at himself. How could I have been so stupid, he was a roamer, he probably smelt another werewolf, got a bit horny and I fell for it. He was probably long gone by now he thought.

"Shit," he said out loud.

He kicked at a clump of grass and winced. Looking down to see his ankle was bruised and swollen. Remembering the night before when he jumped across the road he had badly twisted his ankle. He limped back over to where he had been laying and closed his eyes.

"You stupid, fuckin' moron!" he shouted at himself.

Yeah like a werewolf was going to stay with another, we don't work like that he thought to himself. He opened his eyes and felt the sting of tears in his eyes. He felt so lonely. This was the only part of the gift he didn't like, the isolation. He sat back on the floor and held his head in his hands. Now he had to get back to his apartment, butt naked and without anyone seeing him. This should be fun he thought to himself. He stood and started the long walk back down the valley, he didn't realise he had ended up so high. It was the fun and excitement he thought to himself.

"FUCKIN' BASTARD!" he shouted up the valley, hoping the other was close enough to hear him.

He wasn't and Dean knew it.

He traipsed along the paths, no longer caring whether people saw him or not. His heart was heavy and his head held low. This was not a gift it was a curse, the others were right he thought. You can never have a human partner, how the hell do you explain why you disappear every full moon, you can't tell them the truth. Firstly who would believe it, if they did how they could accept it. It took

24

Dean 2 whole years to come to terms with it and he was the one infected. No, a werewolf could only have a relationship with another werewolf and Deans only chance since he was bitten just went and fucked off. Leaving him alone once again, he started to sob quietly, his grief silent, just as it was with his mentor.

His enhanced hearing heard someone coming along the path, thankfully breaking his train of thought before he got too upset. Dean quickly jumped into the bushes; he was still a werewolf first and foremost. If it only affected him then that was fine, but no it affected the rest of the community, he still had to honour the code. Keep your head down; make acquaintances not friends, leave no trail. He had to honour the code; there was no choice in it. He saw two women walk past him, it was early morning hikers. Luckily it was a Monday so there were only a few who had the time to hike this early. It was terrible on a weekend, more so in holiday season. These forests were famous amongst the hiking community. Soon all that was left of the women were their scents slowly dispersing amid the strong cedar tang. One of the women was wearing a particularly strong perfume. Dean snorted, trying to clear his nose of the overpowering smell. He could taste it at the back of his mouth; he tried to choke it out. No werewolf would ever wear anything with any scent; it was too strong with their powerful sense of smell. They wouldn't be able to smell anything else. Then their noses were useless, and a werewolf with no nose was also useless.

He slipped into town around 7:30, it was just waking. People were getting out of beds across the urban sprawl, paying for those few extra minutes in bed, rushing to get ready for work. He was crouched behind a bush next to a small road that ran behind his apartment complex. He had chosen the building for its position at the edge of town and proximity to the forest. The perfect place for a werewolf to live, easy access to the forest when the change starts to take hold. He took a furtive look around there were no cars coming and there was nobody around. He quickly ran across the road to the fence that surrounds the complex, his building was on the far end. Closer to the city than he liked but that was the only one available at the time. He didn't want to move now, he had just got the place how he wanted it. So he made do. He pushed with his legs and propelled himself over the wooden fence, landing silently on the grass on the other side. All the curtains were drawn on that side, so he would not be seen. He ran across to the building and pushed his back against it, his buttocks cold from the rough concrete. He looked around the corner, it was clear. He crept along the wall, trying to keep below the windows just in case. He got to the end of the building. Not far now he thought. He looked into the square courtyard that lay in the middle of the complex with four buildings along each edge. He scanned the area. There was no one around, he ran across the courtyard as fast as his augmented muscles would allow, dropping onto all fours. He stopped at the main doors and then realised he had no keys. He slipped around to the back; he could still see the claw marks he had made last night.

He extended his claws and climbed up the wall to where he always left a window on the latch, just in case. He slipped his claws underneath the frame and pulled. The window opened with little fuss. He dropped onto his bedroom floor, the thick pile of the carpet warming his feet. He dropped to the floor, lent against the wall and closed his eyes. That was close he thought to himself. He examined his ankle, feeling around for any tell-tale signs of a break. No just badly sprained. He stood and hobbled into the kitchen and over to the fridge, he opened the door and peered inside. He withdrew a bottle of lager and a bag of frozen peas from the freezer compartment. He opened the bottle with one hand and went over to a chair sitting on it wearily. He placed the peas on his ankle, wincing slightly from the sharp cold, sipping his drink. He sank into the chair and relaxed a little.

He couldn't believe he had been so stupid, he had thought his time alone had come to an end. He had hoped he could foster at least a friendship with another werewolf. They would have something in common with one another. But what he really longed for was to have a relationship with a werewolf, they could go for a run together, he wouldn't have to be so alone all the time. He felt a small tear well in his eye. The phone ringing broke him from his thoughts. He limped over to it. Who was ringing at this time he thought. He lifted the receiver.

"Hello?" he said quietly.

"Oh hi Dean, it's Angela from work, just ringing to see if you feel any better," said Angela.

26

"Yeah, I feel a bit better, I think I should be able to return Thursday," said Dean.

"Brill, the boss is going mad over here, he needs you, we have a big contract that's fell behind," her tone almost pleading.

"Well I don't feel well enough to come in today, but Thursday maybe," he hated lying.

"Ok, well I'm happy you feel better, you looked terrible the other day," it was obvious she was concerned.

We always do when the change is coming up he thought.

"It's just a virus," Dean realised he technically wasn't telling a lie.

"Aww, poor baby, do you want me to bring you some soup up tonight," she said sarcastically.

"No I'm alright, I just want to make sure before I come back, I don't want any relapses," he just wanted this conversation to end.

"It's not man flu is it, because I hear it's *really bad*," her tone becoming even more sarcastic.

"No it's not man flu, I've been to the doctors and he said it was a bug that's going round," he said lying.

"Oh sorry I didn't realise," she sounded like a scolded child.

"It's ok, look I will have to go," he didn't want to talk anymore.

"Ok goodbye, see you later," she said hurriedly.

"Yeah bye," Dean sighed.

He replaced the receiver and limped back to the chair; he placed the peas back on his ankle and took another swig of his drink. He lent back and returned to his thoughts. Why was he destined to be alone all the time. His heart longed for something more, for someone more.

He threw the bottle at the kitchen sink, glass and lager raining all over the tiled floor of his kitchenette. Jumping from his chair, he kicked the peas away from him in anger. He paced around the room agitated, ignoring the pain in his ankle. He couldn't believe what he was doing, holding his head in his hands he mentally berated himself for being so stupid again. What was he doing, he thought to himself. What he was doing was wrong; ignoring the code he had been taught. The code he learnt to follow through a terrible tragedy. It is better for him to be alone than for others to be hurt again. He had to remember what happened the last time he didn't follow the code and allowed his heart to lead him. He traipsed into him bedroom and threw himself on his bed. There he curled up and sobbed with a mixture of horror, pain, loneliness and grief. But the overriding emotion however, was one of total confusion over his feelings.

His eyes grew heavy, sleep nagging at the back of his neck and he reluctantly dropped off.

Chapter 4

Awaking five hours later, having fallen asleep through emotional exhaustion. Pulling himself up from his bed he could see he had kicked off his bed clothes in his sleep. Climbing off the bed he gingerly tested his ankle, the muscle was tight and swollen but the pain had lessened greatly. Hobbling through to his living area he saw the destruction he had wrought. A puddle of water surrounded the defrosted bag of peas and glass splinters covered the kitchenette. Slowly he picked his way through the razor sharp obstacle course to one of the cupboards. Taking out a bandage he tip-toed back to the chair where he sat down heavily, his mind weighing him down. He wrapped his ankle up tightly, giving the damaged limb some much needed support. After his first aid he retrieved a brush and began to sweep up the glass. Dumping the resulting detritus into his bin he trudged to his bedroom. Throwing open his wardrobe he quickly dressed in an old pair of jeans and a hole ridden forest green jumper. Pulling on a pair of trainers he ran his fingers through his hair. The bright afternoon sun filled his apartment, but he felt no warmth from it. As though he was dead inside, he came out and left his apartment.

He was walking down the stairs when he saw Val coming up. He could do without someone like her with the mood he was in today.

"Hi Dean what you up to, I thought you had work," she said.

"I'm not very well, I'm going to the chemist to pick up some medication," he feigned a smile.

"Oh I'm sorry to hear that," she said.

"Yes, thank you, I have to dash, I don't want to be out long," he said faking a cough.

"Oh well I'll let you get off then," she said.

"Thanks bye," he said continuing down the stairs.

"Bye," she called after him.

He came to the doors and went out, he had to do something if not he would go mad. So he went through the main gate towards town. He came out on West Forest Crescent, the parking lot to his left. He headed in an easterly direction, along Rectory way. He passed houses to both his left and right. This was where the majority of the people lived in Redridge. It was small town only a population of 1,819 at last count. The houses were all the same, old colonial type, the only thing that didn't fit was his apartment complex. It was the only modern thing in town. There were no work possibilities here due to the fact all the stores were family owned. The old way of doing things were still strong here, the stores were handed down along the family, who run them out of respect for their forebears. So Dean had to find work elsewhere, he did in the next town to the south called Selenbury. It was larger than Redridge and also around 35 miles away, it was better this way; he could keep his life separate. Though the trek was a bit of a pain. He came up to the Old Church, its paint was peeling in places and a few slates were missing from the roof. But it was still intimidating, has been for around 120 years, when the town was founded the first two buildings to go up was the town hall and the church. Dean enjoyed looking into the history of places; you could say he was a history buff. Its spire casting a long shadow due to the dipping sun elongating it, causing it to spread across the road and cover the roundabout in darkness. The cross that sat at its top cast its shadow at the very steps to the town hall. The equally imposing building was well looked after, there was no sign of any peeling paint. Its large wooden columns surpassing both floors and holding a steep apex roof, the windows were the old sash type and its double doors original iron bound hardwood monstrosities.

Dean turned to his left and came to Main Street; the only shops in the whole town were located here. It was the main road into and out of Redridge, along this road was the interstate, but Dean didn't use it very often. He walked past the few shops including the chemist. He stopped outside. He was so deep in his thoughts he hadn't realised this was where he had been heading. Shaking his head he walked away, werewolves never get ill, not even so much as a common cold.

Carrying along Main Street he headed towards the large bridge that spanned the river Prospect. So named for the gold found in its waters during the gold rush in the 1700's, which turned out to be very short lived. He stopped as he reached the middle, leaning on the railing and cast his view along the river. The low sun turning the waters a strange orange-pink hue, even this spectacular view could do little to lighten his sullen mood. His depression sinking to an all-time low, closing his eyes he listened to the low babble of the gently flowing river beneath him. He began to absorb into his own thoughts. He didn't want to be alone anymore however he knew the council forbade unions outside of their enclaves. His thoughts drifted to the other from last night. He needed him, his body lusted for him and his very soul craved him. Last night was amazing for Dean, not just the sex, but for him to have companionship with another of his kind. He was just so lonely; all he wanted was someone to spend his life with. It felt as though he was caught up in a hurricane of emotions. His head said no, his heart said yes and his soul bridged the gap between. He just didn't know what to do. A car rushing past shook him from his thoughts. His gaze wandered along the river to Old MacArthur Park, he could see a baseball game being played. From the colours he could see it was the town's school team playing another town. He tried to see the score but it was too far away, the numbers were nothing but a yellow blur. With a blink, his eyes magnified and focused the image. The score was 34-12 to the home team; the others were losing by a large margin. He smirked slightly at his visual advantage over humans. Even through all the loneliness and anguish he still loved being a werewolf. He decided to watch the game for a little bit, till it was time for him to get ready for the last change. He continued along the bridge and entered the park. A scent caught his attention, pricking a glint of familiarity from his memory.

He continued towards the baseball diamond, the scent growing stronger with each step. He sniffed a couple more times trying to discern the reason he recognized the scent. He didn't know why but the scent had certainly picked his interest deep in his subconscious. He walked along till he got to a nearly empty bleacher and sat two rows from the back. The game was going well, the home town team's lead had grown by a further two points. His mind drifted backwards in his memories, back to his childhood. To a happier, less complicated time. To the time he hit his first home run when he was thirteen. The pride his dad felt at that moment was almost tangible. Then he remembered what was to happen just six years from that point. The happiness was not to last, he tore the thought from his mind. The last thing he needed right now was to be reminded of the time his world came crashing down. He heard someone walk past him on the top bench. This was strange because there was no one there earlier. Then the smell hit him, strong male pheromones, certainly werewolf in origin. He turned quickly and lifted his nose to the air, teasing out the details from the scent. It was a werewolf he knew; it was the one from last night. He scanned the area quickly, looking for any sign of him. It was then he realised he had no idea how this other looked in his human form. He could be any of the men that were walking around the area. He stood and followed the scent, he followed the path a little while till the scent lessened, and he retraced his steps and carried along from there. The smell was getting stronger now, he was closing in, the human part of his heart jumped at the possibility of meeting him again, and the wolf part revelled in the hunt. He followed the scent right up to the bank of the river that ran through the town. It stopped, just stopped right at the edge of the bank. It was obvious he was playing with him like the previous night. Turning to his left towards the bridge he walked a few paces and stopped. Sniffing a couple of times his glands told him the scent had dissipated. So walking back along the bank he picked up the trail once more. He carried walking along the bank, only concerned by the smell that now filled his nostrils. He continued till he got to the bridge not far from his apartment complex. The smell was getting even stronger now; his mind was awash with the intricacies of this unknown person. He leapt on to the bridge from the bank, his nose close to the floor, his primal side taking over. He was so engrossed in the smell that he had dropped onto all fours with his nose to the ground, like a blood hound searching for its quarry. He soon realised what he was doing and quickly returned to his discreet tracking. The scent led around to the front of his apartment complex. Stopping at the main gate his head cocked to one side, the features etched with confusion. Taking in another sniff he smelt for the trail, this was defiantly where the other werewolf had been.

He followed the scent to his building; climbing the stairs the smell began to grow even stronger. When he got to his door he realised this was the origin of the scent, but there was no one around. It was then that he noticed the tied plastic bag at the foot of his door. He bent over and picked it up. Bringing it closer to his nose he sniffed at it. The smell was unbearable, physically knocking him backwards as his olfactory glands were overwhelmed with the many details of this person. Weaved within and through the strong heady musk of this other male his own scent mingled. Though far weaker he could pick out his own pheromones. Swiftly he unlocked the door and burst in, throwing the bag onto the coffee table he glanced around hoping he would be hid somewhere.

"Why would he be hiding in my apartment," he said to the emptiness, shaking his head.

Throwing himself onto the sofa he stared intently at the bag now resting on the empty coffee table. He lifted it up, noticing it was surprisingly light. Carefully he untied the knot before turning it out onto the table below. A smile spread across his face when he saw the contents. It was his clothes he had ripped off last night, when the change had took over. He lifted out his shirt; it was almost split down the middle, one of the arms ripped clean off. His jeans were in a worst state, ripped to complete shreds. Bits of them were strewn across the table's surface. When he lifted up a particularly large piece of denim from the table, something was underneath it. It was a piece of white paper, a note. He lifted the note from the table, the stench was amazing. He sniffed at it tentatively, screwing up his eyes from the strength. It was saturated with his scent, no wonder he was able to follow it so easy. He read the note.

> *Dear young sir,*
> *You know you really shouldn't leave things around for anybody to happen upon. It's lucky I followed your scent, who knows what could have happened. I do apologize for the communication, I didn't mean to it was done subconsciously. I smelt your stimulating scent the night before and I haven't been with another werewolf for so long. I was thinking about you and well you know what happened next. What happened shouldn't have, but I'm glad it did. It was amazing.*
> *Sorry for leaving it was inconsiderate of me, however I didn't want to complicate things. One more night of the lunar cycle, hope I will see you again. And maybe we can see each other outside of the cycle.*
>
> *You're Conqueror*

Dean smiled as he read the note again, his eyes lighting up.

Just the thought of him made him happy and he hadn't been happy for such a long time. He was unsure of what to do with regards to this other werewolf. His emotions warred within him again, but a new emotion had joined in. Hate. He hated what he was, hated the rules he was forced to follow. But most of all he hated himself for what he did. The horrors off that night once again filled his subconscious, the screams, the blood, the fear and guilt. A strangled wail of pain escaped his paralysed throat as he heard the loud echo of the gunshot that would destroy all he held dear. He became empty, devoid of everything but guilt and horror. Had he paid penance for his crime? He didn't know, but he knew he would have forgiven him. His dear Ale........ he couldn't even bring himself to think his name. The pain was too great. Perhaps he did deserve to be happy once again; after all he had lived his life in isolation for many years. Fearing to become close to someone, to lose them through his own selfishness and stupidity, he had matured so much, being nothing more than a child back then. Having lost everything, even his humanity, it was too much to experience at such a young age and remain sane. He wasn't going to allow his past to ruin his future, he had paid enough. The werewolf council be damned if they thought ancient rules were going to ruin his life any longer. This revelation eased his mind; he didn't have to follow the rules. After all he didn't ask for this it was forced upon him. He lent back on the sofa and put his feet on the coffee table. Pressing the note to his nose he inhaled the other scent deeply. He let out a lustful sigh as animalistic pleasure shuddered throughout his body. The scent was just so alluring, he wanted him right here right now. He wanted to go and find him right now and tell him they could be together forever, even though he knew it was wrong. He read the last bit again. Who did he think he was conqueror indeed? Didn't he realise Dean had surrendered himself over to him. The only thing he could do was to wait till tonight and hope he could find him. He put the note back on the coffee table and picked up all his ripped clothes. He put them back in the plastic bag and tied it up again. Lifting the bag he carried it to his bin and dropped it inside, the glass on the bottom rattled. Glancing at the clock on the wall it showed it to be 3:30pm and the sun had begun to dip further behind the mountains. It would not be long, but it was too long for Dean. He decided to have a little sleep before tonight. If last night was anything to go on, he was going to need his rest.

35

The digital clock beside his bed cast a reddish light over the room. It showed the time to be 10:30pm. Dean rolled onto his bare stomach and stretched out his weary limbs. Yawning loudly as he stared out the uncovered window. It was now dark, the moon revealing itself from behind the shadowy clouds. He hadn't slept only tossed and turned, his excitement about the impending mid night rendezvous barely contained. He swung his legs out of bed and sat upon its edge. Standing once again stretching out his fullness, revealing his bare, smooth body to the silver round orb that hung above. He basked in its light, feeling warmth and peace spread from his heart to the very tips of his fingers. His skin tingled at the lights caress. He felt an ache start in his joints and his muscles grew tight, the change had begun. He pulled on the discarded clothes from earlier foregoing his underwear. Slipping some trainers on his bare feet he grabbed his bag and slipped out of the apartment. Closing the door as quietly as he could and padding down the concrete stairs. Leaving behind a shallow echo as his footfalls resounded off the stark walls of the narrow stairwell. He ran through the doors and into the cool night air. It smelt of the forest, a scent that almost beckoned him, begging him to return, to return home. He quickly trotted through the gate and towards the edge of the forest. Its stillness was most inviting. As he crossed the threshold he exhaled a sigh, this was his natural habitat. Adjusting his backpack he walked deeper and deeper into darkness.

Chapter 5

Choosing a small clearing deep enough into the forest he began to strip. As he pulled off his jumper the cold night air bit into his exposed flesh, goose bumps popping up over the exposed surface. Kicking off his trainers he let his bare feet sink into the damp cool earth, this was how he should be. Connected to mother earth. Unbuttoning his jeans he let them fall to his ankles before stepping out of them. He quickly scooped up the vestiges of his false human life and stuffed them unceremoniously into the plastic bag along with the discarded backpack. Sealing it up with the herb tied elastic band and secreted it in a bed of ferns. He sat down on the floor and waited for the change to start. As it turned out he didn't have too long to wait, soon he felt the aching and tightness once again. It was about to start. Thankfully this time, it was not in overdrive so it was a lot less painful. He relaxed his muscles and let the change take its course. He soon burst from the clearing in his wolf form, with long shaggy golden blonde coat and bright blue eyes conveying a deep emotion and intelligence. Lifting his nose to the air; he tested for any sign of the other. There was none. It didn't mean he wasn't going to show up; werewolves don't all change at the same time. Sometimes it is delayed, sometimes it is accelerated. He ran off into the forest hoping he would find the other from last night.

He searched and searched but there was no sign of him, not one single fragment of a scent. When his stomach began to growl in earnest he abandoned his search but he didn't want to hunt. He just wanted HIM. Yet again he was left alone, a lone werewolf in a world of humans. He whimpered sadly as a wave of depression spread over him. He wanted to curl up in a ball but his animal side forced him to hunt for a meal, he quickly found another rabbit and gulped it down in haste. After finishing his short meal he ran up a hill, coming to a small outcropping where he let loose the loudest and most drawn out howl he could muster. It was laden with his own forlornness. Desperation forcing him to continue till his vocal chords became sore, his final howl coming out as a hoarse whisper. He listened intently for any sound of a reply, but there was none. Giving up he slowly trudged into the silent woods in search of some water to ease his throat. After a little while he came upon a babbling brook and lapped away at the cool refreshing water. Walking away he slumped on the bank and curled up in a tight ball closing his eyes. Wishing to lose himself in the oblivion that was sleep, he

38

remembered the last time he felt this bad, it was the time he found his mentor dead, and he had stayed with his body till daybreak. At which point he had to leave. He had been shot by a human one night and in a fit of rage Dean had done unspeakable things .When he had changed back into his human form he carried his mentor's body home and burned down their lodge. He was Dean's best friend, the man who helped him come to grips with his gift. Now he was gone, just like the other. Just left him to be alone for the rest of his life, if he could cry he would. But just like with his mentor he couldn't, he had no tear ducts. He just drifted into a depressive sleep.

He awoke the next morning once again in his human form, stretching out his body, the joints popping as they realigned themselves into their original position. Shuffling forwards he knelt at the edge of the stream and washed his face clean off blood. Throwing the cold water in his face in an attempt to rid the sleep that still nagged at the back off his eyes. He saw some small ripples in the water as though it was spitting with light rain. It took him a few moments to realise it was him, crying spontaneously. He fell backwards, lying on the hard pebbles. Tears coming more freely now, he felt so alone.

"There's no need to cry," came a soft and compassionate male voice from behind him, spoken with a flawless English accent.

Dean jumped up, claws slipping from their sheaths involuntarily, his animal side taking a defensive posture, ready to attack this unknown person. Dean's eyes widened at the sight that lay before him. At the crest of the incline stood a man slightly older than himself, his naked body gleamed in the dawns rays. Its soft light playing over the short jet black hairs that covered his broad muscular chest, continuing down his heavily muscled stomach coming to a point amongst his pubic hair. This in turn surrounded a large and thick organ that hung lazily above his sizable testicles. Dean tore his eyes from the man's package and stared up at his face. The facial features were hard but yet had a subtle softness to them. His vivid green eyes twinkled in the sun, as though they were faceted emeralds set in the marble face of Michelangelo's David. They shone warm and affectionately, his jet black hair hung loose and cascaded down one shoulder. He was beautiful. He smelt of unbridled sexual prowess and masculinity. Dean recognized the scent immediately, it was the other werewolf.

"You!" was all Dean could muster.

The other smiled broadly and nodded in way of a greeting, "My name is Edmund Whitlock, what is yours young one?"

"I'm Dean Johnson, where the hell was you last night?" his sadness turning into a spark of anger.

Edmunds smile dropped when he saw the dampness on Dean's cheeks, it was obvious he had hurt him, "I'm sorry, I heard you howling but I couldn't reach you with damnable interstate!"

"Oh I didn't realise," he said apologetically.

"So when I awoke I decided to come and find you. I couldn't just leave you again," Edmund look directly into Deans eyes and he knew he was sincere.

"Thank you," Dean was on the verge of tears again.

Edmund didn't say anything he just walked straight at Dean and grabbed him by the back of his neck, pulling him close. Dean let his hands roam over the other man's body; his muscles were taught and hard. Their lips locked in flaming passion, tongues thrusting deep. Their bare skin rubbing against one another's, the feeling so sensual and intimate, heating their already alight fire. Dean's eyes shone with a brightness that looked as though two blue stars had replaced his eyes. They held a great sorrow about them, but also a longing. His smile was just as stunning almost intoxicating, like it was the first time he had truly smiled for a very long time. This young man was amazing and took Edmunds breath away. He lifted Dean off the floor and laid him down on the wet grass. His strong, toned body pressed close to Dean's slender frame. Edmund kissed at Dean's tender neck, moving his way towards his ear. Where he gave the lobe a playful nip and caused a giggle of pleasure from its owner, before whispering in his ear.

"This time we are going to do this right, take our time."

With that Dean caught Edmund unawares and rolled him onto his back, kissing his way down his body. Licking his rock hard pecs, nibbling at the nipples before brushing his lips over his abs, moving even lower. Edmunds penis had become hard, its bulbous head large and round. Dean gently kissed the tip, tasting the saltiness. He slowly, agonizingly licked along the entire length. Edmund moaned as he encircled the head with his lips, feeling its thickness, its heat as he took in another inch of his hard member. Soon he had the whole length in his mouth, its silky smooth head touching the back of his throat; he gave it a deep hard suck. Bobbing his head up and down, slowly at first, but soon speeding up, he licked along the slit, tasting the pre-come. Edmund had his head back, grunting and groaning whilst he caressed Dean's neck and played with his ears. As Dean's saliva moistened Edmunds meat and his lips slipped up and down much easier, he began to explore Edmunds body. Clenching his rock hard buns, slipping a finger in his crack, teasing his hole, Edmund groaned louder at the extra attention.

Edmund put his middle finger in his mouth and began to suck on it. He then pulled Dean (who was very intent on his penis) up so that their faces were level. Dean cuddled up to his hunky body, feeling his own hard on trapped between their bodies. They kissed one another hard. Edmund ran his hands along Dean's back, caressing the smooth firm skin. His hands moved lower as they headed for his pert, tight buttocks. Kneading them slowly he parted the cheeks, before carefully rubbing Dean's small nub of flesh with his lubricated finger. Greasing it up enough, he confidently pushed it in. Dean gave a small squeal as he began to work his finger in and out of his hole. Slipping in another finger, Edmund began to move his fingers around inside him, twisting. Dean squealed louder, growing higher pitched each time Edmund touched the right spot. Once Deans hole was pliable enough to accept his girth he removed his finger with a pop, leaving the hole kissing at the air. Dean knew what was coming next, this was what he was waiting for, and he flipped over so he was lying on his front. Spreading his legs to allow access to his hole, he felt Edmunds heavyweight physique bearing down upon his boyish frame.

Edmund pressed the head on target which was soon fully engulfed. Dean concentrated on relaxing his muscles, breathing deeply. Holding onto his hips Edmund lifted Dean slightly and pushed deeper. Gently, he eased in the last few remaining inches. Taking a firm hold of Dean's slim shoulders he began to rock his hips slowly building up a steady rhythm. With each inward motion Dean let out a small gasp. The penetration growing deeper as Edmund began to rock faster. Dean's gasps became lust filled moans of pure pleasure. Edmund built up speed and ferocity, his grunts becoming more and more animalistic, verging on a bestial growl.

Edmund reached beneath Dean's body and took a hold of his hard penis. He began to stroke at it slowly, the rod growing hotter in his grasp. Stopping occasionally to tease its sensitive tip.

Then suddenly Edmund pushed as much of himself into Dean as he could. Dean could feel the throb of Edmunds crown against his anal walls, before his load coated his insides. Edmund released a long drawn out moan of complete and utter pleasure. As he was brought to climax, he sped up his hand job. Edmund wrapped his arm tightly around Dean's fresh, young body as he gently fucked the last few drops from his scrotum.

"Fuck the rules," Dean screamed as he basked in the warmth of Edmunds masculine embrace.

Dean could feel his insides stir as his own climax built up. Dean threw his head back and shrieked as he spurted jets and jets of come all over Edmunds hand. Even after its eruption had ceased Dean's crown still throbbed in between Edmunds sticky fingers. Edmund withdrew, his penis drooping at half-mast. Dean rolled onto his back gasping for breath, watching Edmund lick the remnants of his spunk from his fingers.

"Yum," he said devilishly.

They lay together for a while, Deans head resting on Edmunds chest, arm draped over his body. Dean could hear Edmunds heart beating in his manly chest. He felt contented, like the other night. But he found himself wondering if this was such a good idea as doubts began to creep in.

"What did you say earlier?" asked Edmund as he stroked

Dean's hair.

"I said fuck the rules," his reply quiet.

Edmund chuckled softly, "Well we could, but I would much prefer fucking you."

"Behave," Dean giggled playfully slapping the other man's bare chest.

"What? The rules on fraternization outside the enclaves is archaic at best and should be abolished," his voice calm as he stroked Deans bare bicep.

"Yeah but it is still a rule, a law really. We should still follow it, there could be consequences if we didn't," the doubts in his own head became stronger as he came down of his lust fuelled high.

"Oh please. what are they going to do? Exile you from the werewolf nation?" he looked directly into Dean's eyes as he continued, "You don't even live within the nation, and you live with humans. So what does it matter if we break a few ancient rules?"

"No, no we can't!" Dean suddenly jumped up and walked away.

"Dean why are you so against this?" Edmund rose slowly and followed him.

"Look I just know what can happen when you don't follow the rules," he spun round suddenly, sadness in his eyes.

"Come to me," Edmund held his arms open invitingly.

Dean stepped into the bigger man's grasp and felt the large arms encircle him. He felt safe here, but more than that he felt as though it was right, almost like it was destined to be. He threw his own arms round Edmunds body and pulled him closer. His corded muscles growing taught at the prospect of losing him. He wished to all that was divine that he would stay in these arms forever. Unbeknown to him, Edmund was getting the same feelings of destiny. He had an undeniable urge to be close to him, it was something he had never felt before. Maybe this is what true love felt like he thought to himself. His grip growing tighter.

"Look Dean I've been a werewolf a very long time and I have never heard of werewolves becoming mates causing any trouble," his tone soft and soothing, "Can you in your young years dispute that?"

"Well no, but....." Dean began.

"There are no buts, are you happy being with me?" asked Edmund.

Dean sighed and whispered a quiet yes into Edmunds chest. He had no idea how happy he felt, his heart sang and his body was filled with warmth.

"Then isn't that all that should matter?" he asked, "And not the rules of people who have never met you?"

Dean nodded with his head pressed up against the other man's strong beating heart. It was half an answer to the question and half a realisation that he could be happy with this man. But only if he accepted his past and the first step to that was for him to admit it.

"Edmund there is something you need to hear first," Dean started to say before he was silenced with a playful nip on his rump.

"I believe our life stories can wait till we are both dressed. Don't you agree?" the other man said quickly.

Dean laughed when he realised they were both stood totally naked in the middle of the forest with the sun rising higher. But Edmund was right, if he was happy then that should be the only thing that matters. He was also right about the clothes. They released one another from their fierce embrace.

"You're not going to disappear again are you?" Dean asked his eyes pleading.

"No my dear, I don't intend to leave for a while yet," his smile was playful but his eyes serious.

They kissed lightly before going their separate ways; Dean walked backwards keeping his eyes on the other man's rock hard buns. He couldn't wait to get his hands on them again. But first he needed to get dressed and to get them both back to his apartment. So lifting his nose to the air he started the hunt for his clothes. Picking up the scent almost immediately, he ran through the undergrowth following his nose like he had been taught. Finding his clothes he quickly dressed, hurrying to see his lover again. He walked to one of the paths and waited for Edmund to arrive. He knew it may take a while as he had said he was across the interstate. So he paced up and down the footpath, his body fidgeting. He turned quickly when he heard heavy footfalls and smiled when he saw Edmund running over the brow of the hill. Even though fully dressed he still looked formidable. His broad chest barely contained within the light blue shirt he wore. He was panting lightly by the time he reached Dean.

"Not as fit as you used to be? Well you are getting old," Dean teased.

Edmund replied with a stare and a swat on Dean's bottom. Who rubbed the sore cheek.

"How old are you exactly? You never said," Dean asked, genuinely curious.

"Well I'm one hundred and forty six years old," he answered casually, "What about you, mid-fifties?"

Deans eyes widened, "Erm no, I'm twenty six," embarrassment in his voice.

Edmund looked at Dean before shaking his head, "I have become a cradle snatcher!"

Dean giggled and pushed the older man, "I'm not that young!"

Edmund smiled and put his arm round Deans shoulders holding him close as his fellow werewolf wound his arm round Edmunds back, "Come on let's get you home, I think we could both do with some sleep."

Dean snaked his hand into Edmunds jeans and clenched the hard defined globe he found there, "Sleep wasn't what I had in mind," he said sultrily.

Edmund laughed a great deep bellow of amusement that made his eyes dance as he pulled his young lover closer. He soon began to realise just how much he felt for Dean. Almost like love at first sight. They didn't say anything for the rest of the journey, just walked with their arms wrapped around one another. It wasn't long before they were stood outside Dean's apartment

"You've already been here haven't you," it was more a statement than a question.

"Oh you got the package did you?" Edmund grinned.

"Yeah, thanks, I don't think I will get you're stink out of my apartment for a while," he feigned annoyance but in truth he loved Edmunds scent.

"Well, get used to it, you will never get it out now," he wiggled his eyebrows at Dean causing the younger man to giggle.

Dean pulled Edmund closer and planted an almighty kiss on his eager lips. Dean quickly opened the door and ushered Edmund inside. He told him to sit down. Edmund sat on the sofa and took off his boots, putting them under the coffee table. Taking in a sniff; he could still smell Dean on his body. He smiled at the smell.

Dean went into the kitchen and opened the fridge. Taking out a couple of objects he returned to Edmund and held them both up.

"Whipped cream or chocolate sauce," he said smiling and winking.

Edmund gave Dean a toothy grin, revealing his oversized

canines giving him a malevolent look. His vivid green eyes shone with mischievousness, as he spoke one single word.

"Both."

Chapter 6

His heart was beating heavily in his chest; his lungs were beginning to tighten with the strenuous exercise. He had to carry on but it was starting to get hard to breath. A shot rang out through the forest. Hearing men shouting and swearing, there was another shot this one closer to him. He could hear their voices but he couldn't understand them from this distance. Every part of his mind and body was concerned only with survival. The hunters were behind him, but they couldn't keep up with a werewolf. He was starting to build up a sizable lead on the humans. Catching a flash of grey out of the corner of one eye. He stole a quick glance to his right; he could see the bushes move and glimpses of grey fur through the gaps. He was glad he had gotten away too. The worry he had felt since the hunt began now subsided.

There was another shot; Dean heard it whistle past his ear. There was a loud yip as of a wounded animal and he could see the grey shape slumped to the ground.

"ALEXIUS!" he shouted out.

He sat bolt upright in bed. Sweat was covering his entire body like a musty damp film. His heart was beating so heavily that his body throbbed with its pulse.

"Dean are you ok?" he heard a voice to his left.

He looked over to see Edmund sitting in bed next to him, eyeing him concerned. It was clear from his features he was worried about him. He reached out a hand to him, Dean flinched and recoiled.

"Please don't," his voice cracking.

"Dean what's the matter?" asked Edmund his eyes fixed on Dean intently.

"Oh Edmund, it was a dream, a dream from the past and one I thought I had forgotten," Dean replied.

"Dean what do you mean?" Edmunds worried eyes were fixed on Dean.

49

"Oh Edmund it was a nightmare, one I never thought I'd have again," he replied.

"What do you mean?" Edmund placed a comforting hand on Dean's trembling shoulder.

"It was the night Alexius died, the night he was murdered and the night I became a murderer," Dean sobbed, holding his head as he finished the sentence and a great shame washed over him.

"What do you mean a murderer and who is Alexius?" Edmunds face became etched with confusion.

"I.......I don't want to talk about it at the moment, just hold me please," Dean was clearly disturbed about something.

Edmund reached over and placed his arms around Dean, pulling him close. Dean laid his head on Edmunds strong shoulder and wept silently. All the while the other man stroked his hair, comforting him as best as he could. They both lay down and Dean snuggled up closer to his lover, feeling secure for the first time in many years. Edmund held him close till the tears slowed. Looking at Dean; his cheeks were streaked with tears, a damp patch forming on the pillow case. He kissed him lightly on the forehead.

"Are you alright?" he asked keeping his tone soft.

Dean smiled weakly but said nothing.

"Dean, if this relationship is to work you have to open up to me, you can trust me you know. You're no longer alone, please allow me to share some of your burden," Edmund said pleading with Dean to open up.

"Thank you, you don't know how good it feels for someone to say that, I've been alone for such a long time," Dean said his smile looking more genuine.

"Dean I will always be there for you, I swear to you," Edmund said.

Dean said nothing but just hugged Edmund more tightly. They lay there in a warm embrace for what seemed a lifetime before Dean finally broke the silence.

"Alexius was.............well for lack of a better word.............my father."

"I don't under....stand," said Edmund.

"Well I think you need to know a few things about me Edmund," Dean said sitting up.

"Go on," said Edmund.

Dean swung out of bed and pulled on a pair of jeans that were beside the bed where he had left them that morning. Walking through to the kitchen he poured two cups of luke warm coffee, placed then on the coffee table and sat waiting for Edmund. He knew he would follow him out. A few moments later Edmund came out of the bedroom likewise wearing the trousers from this morning. Dean rubbed at his chest; it was still sticky from the chocolate sauce earlier. Edmund sat down on the sofa next to Dean; he draped one arm around the back of the sofa resting his hand on Dean's bare shoulder. He picked up the coffee and sipped at it.

"So, what do you need to tell me?" asked Edmund.

"Right I suppose I should start from the beginning," said Dean quietly.

"Look Dean if you don't want to do this now, then that's fine by me," said Edmund.

"No.........no I have to tell you, you have a right to know, besides if I don't tell you now I never will." said Dean.

"Ok, if you are sure," said Edmund.

Dean just nodded.

"Well it all began about seven years ago, when I was bitten," Dean said, "I was out with some friends when a pack of pure werewolves attacked us in the forest. Most died except for me, God I was in a bad way. I was seriously mutilated, practically ripped to pieces but that was the night I first met Alexius."

Edmund just nodded his head for him to continue.

Dean began by telling about the night he was attacked.

Dean waited until his parents were asleep, he heard his father begin to snore. The sound was deep and loud, he knew this was his time. He swung out of bed, already fully dressed and tip toed over to his wardrobe trying to miss the creaky floorboards. He opened the doors and took out a pair of old trainers, he pulled them on quickly. He snuck over to the window and slowly eased it open, taking care not to make the old sash mechanism squeak too much. It didn't work, a loud squeak issued from the cables on the pulleys. It echoed throughout the house. Dean jumped as he heard movement in the other room, he listened intently for any sign the noise had awoken them. He heard his father cough and roll back over, he was safe enough. He swung his leg over the window sill; straddling it he threw his other leg over and dropped onto the floor below. The cold night air enveloped him, its stinging touch biting at the exposed skin on his arms. He looked up at the sky, the full moon slowly revealing itself from the clouds. The moonlight was adequate to navigate to the meeting point; Dean hoped he would not be late. He looked at his watch, it showed 11:30. He was cutting it close.

He walked through the streets of his home town as quickly as he could. His head turning sharply at any sound he heard, he didn't like the night much, especially not alone. He made his way along the roads towards the forest that ran along one edge of the town. As he got closer to the forest he could hear voices, people were laughing and joking. He knew he was almost there. He was excited to be there, it was the first party in the woods he had been invited to. It happened each year around the same time and only the most popular students were invited. They were all from different schools and colleges. He had been so happy when he received the paper in his locker. Cutting down a dingy alley between two buildings he came out the other end and could see them stood around in their own little groups. Talking and gossiping with one another, girls were giggling and the lads were laughing and pushing others around. He could never understand why they had to do all that macho crap, it was a foreign concept to him. He slowly walked up the hill furtively looking around for anyone he knew. He kept his head down. When a shadow covered him, he looked up to see that it was a man. He was built like a body builder; his thick neck almost disappeared in the mass of his shoulder muscles. Dean smiled at the man who merely scowled at him.

"You gotta' invite, cause if not you're not comin' any further," the man said, his voice like gravel.

"Yeah, of course I have," Dean said quickly.

He fished around in his back pocket for his invite, ripping the piece of paper free. He passed it to the man, his hand shaking. The man looked at the paper and eyed Dean menacingly. He passed the paper back to Dean standing to one side and waved him along. Dean hurried up the hill, trying not to look behind him. He looked at each group of people as he passed by, looking for his friends. Spotting them at the far end of the throng, close to the forest's edge he sped up. One of the girls from his circle of friends saw him approach.

"Dean, I didn't know you were invited," she called to him.

"Yeah, just got the invite today at college," he called back.

They all turned and greeted him. He smiled at them, waving and shaking hands. Then he saw him, the lad he had fancied since the first moment he had clapped eyes on him. His hair shone in the moonlight, each strand catching the soft dull glow, falling around his magnificent eyes, which in turn glinted with an inner mischievousness. His perfect lips curled up in a smile as he saw Dean. He chuckled slightly when he saw the way that Dean was looking at him.

"Hi Dean," the boy said giving him a little wink.

"Hi James," was all Dean could manage.

53

He could hardly think, his mouth was becoming dry and all he could see was James in front of him smiling. He felt a hand on his shoulder; he spun around to see who it was.

"Dean are you alright?" asked a familiar voice.

"Y.....yes I'm fine thanks Mel," he said.

"You seemed to go into a little world of your own there," she smirked.

"Yeah I suppose I did," he said absently, his eyes drawn back to James.

"Mmmm, and I think I can guess what's happening in that world as well," she laughed.

Dean didn't hear her; he was so engrossed in looking at James. He was talking to some other girls from Dean's college, obviously telling a joke from the way the girls were giggling. Even the way he laughed was beautiful to Dean, so elegant and refined. Not like the muscle bound jocks he had seen earlier, whooping and shouting like idiots. Being with James was like being with royalty; he had that air about him. Everything that he did was with grace and purpose. The way he dressed, so perfect, each piece of his outfit put together to complement as a whole. To Dean he was just that, perfect.

There was a lot of shouting and cheering off to his right, he tore his eyes from James to look at what was happening. He could see that in the distance people were walking into the woods, the party in the woods had started. Soon they would be led to a secluded and secret area, where there would be a large bonfire, beer and some tents to sleep in when the partying was over. Dean was very excited as was everyone. Dean's group began to follow the others, James was just ahead of him, and he glanced at his tight buttocks. He was mesmerised by the way his fine arse swayed with each step he took.

"Why don't you ask him out?" asked Mel

"W....what, sorry Mel I was miles away," his mind was elsewhere.

"No you weren't, you were staring at his arse," she said.

"I was not," Dean tried to defend himself.

"Yes you were, why don't you just ask him out and have done with it, you've been swooning over him for months now," she said exasperated.

"What could he see in me, look at him Mel, look at how perfect he is, why would he be interested in me," Dean said.

Mel slapped him round the head lightly.

"You are going to ask him out tonight, or I 'am, it's about time you had a boyfriend Dean," said Mel.

"I've had boyfriends," Dean said.

"I mean a real boyfriend, not a casual shag," her voice turning stern.

"Ok," Dean said.

"Really? Cause if not I will be," she said.

"Yes, yes I will honest, I know what he will say though, he'll probably laugh at me," he shook his head.

"You may be surprised," she said cryptically.

They continued to follow the other people into the woods. Only a select few know the exact spot where the party will be held. The people who were invited are given a meeting place only. When it is time the ones who know the place will lead the others into the woods. Dean's group was in the middle. He could hear people chattering excitedly, he had to admit he was excited. It showed that he was popular with a lot of people; the party in the woods was a very exclusive. Though it was not allowed to have a party in the woods as it was a protected site it went ahead every year anyway. The police had tried to stop it a couple of years back, they failed spectacularly. So they decided to just let it go. Dean didn't know whether that was because they had failed before, or because the parents of a lot of the kids who went were very powerful. Dean didn't really care he was just happy to be there.

He saw a couple of lads further up the line start pushing one another, soon breaking out in a small scuffle. Two girls who seemed to be their girlfriends tried to pull them apart but with little success. One of the girls fell to the floor as she was inadvertently pushed over. She fell in the soft ground, getting covered in sludge and screamed. The shrill noise soon broke the guys out of their posturing. The girl stood and slapped her boyfriend across the face before storming off back into town. Her boyfriend called to her and ran after her, trying to apologize. Each time he tried she just screamed louder. Dean looked back up the line at the other guy who had got into the fight. He was arguing with his girlfriend now, who seemed to be defending the other girl. They must be friends Dean thought. He raised his voice which just infuriated her even more; she started to scream obscenities at him. Calling him every name under the sun. It was clear the lad was also getting mad; the argument got even more heated. The lad snapped and gave the girl a backhand slap. There was a gasp from everyone who was watching, Dean saw some of the other guys in the crowd moving towards the lad. But his girlfriend wasn't going to take that. After the initial shock had worn off, she looked at him with the most hatred. She grabbed him by the shoulders and brought her knee up to his groin. Everyone gave out an Oooo in almost perfect unison. The lad grabbed at his privates and dropped to his knees as the wind was knocked out of him. Soon people started to laugh at him. The girl spat in his face and too walked off towards town. She left the lad lying on the wet ground, groaning with pain.

"That has got to hurt," Dean said grimacing.

"Well you know what they say about a woman scorned," James chuckled.

The crowd soon got moving again, laughing as they passed

the lad still on the floor cradling his pride as much as his privates. As they passed the lad on the floor, both Dean and James looked at him, trying not to laugh. Dean could hear Mel giggling from behind him. He looked up at the sky, the moon was full and bright and not a cloud in the sky. He was nearing the forest's edge, its deep shadows almost sapping every drop of light the moon could emit. He knew his eyes would adjust after a while, but those few moments he has always dreaded. He felt someone's arm encircle his; it was James clinging to his arm pulling him closer. Dean could see an anxious expression come across his face. The realisation that James was scared off the dark too emboldened his resolve. His back straightened and his nerves hardened. He walked into the forest with all the confidence and bravado he could muster. When there was a strange noise instead of shrieking like he normally would he just pulled James closer smiling comfortingly at him. This time he would be the knight in shining armour instead of the damsel in need of rescue. He felt Mel put her hand on his shoulder as she passed them both, casting a half smile at Dean knowingly. Dean was sure she knew he was about as scared as James was. But so long as James didn't know was all that mattered. He could see flickering lights up ahead, they were getting close.

They came out of the forest and were confronted with an awesome sight. There was a clearing almost 30m across, filled with all the other people he had seen waiting earlier. They were already starting to drain one of the many kegs that were piled up at one end. James let go of Deans arm and smiled at him, he pulled Dean close and kissed him lightly on the cheek. A shiver ran down Dean's body as his lips touched his skin, like an electric current.

"Thanks," James whispered in his ear, his breath tickling the small minute hairs that grew on its surface.

Dean could only smile, the shock knocking him silent. James winked at Dean and walked away into the gathering crowd, leaving him still dumbstruck. His smile did not fading. Soon the sound of music came from the left, quiet at first but soon becoming louder as the D.J fiddled with the sound levels.

Chapter 7

Later that night Dean was lent against a tree watching the rest of the people dancing. Passing his gaze over them, he shook his head at the way some where acting. His gaze lingered a while when he saw a fit guy. Catching movement out the corner of his left eye he turned his head to see Mel striding straight for him. He knew what she wanted, but he just didn't feel like it at the moment.

"Mel I don't want to dance right now," he insisted before she even had time to open her mouth.

"Dean it's a bloody party you imbecile, dancing is what you are supposed to do," she said.

"Mel I just don't want to," he insisted.

"Dean you're my best friend, and I love you to bits, but get the fuck over there and dance will you," she shouted over the music.

"You're just going to keep nagging me aren't you?" he asked.

She nodded, staring at him.

Dean smiled and gave up, he knew he wouldn't win. So he trudged over to where they were all dancing, picking his way through the revellers bumping into a few as they threw themselves around to the music. He could almost feel Mel's eyes on him as she glared at his back; he couldn't get away with it this time. He couldn't just slope of into a corner like he would usually do. The truth was he was shy, but with Mel here he would have to 'mingle' as she always put it. Basically she meant flirt. So he began to sway his hips to the music, catching the beat and rhythm immediately. Mel knew he was a fantastic dancer; he just lacked the confidence to believe it.

His body moved in a fluid like movement, swaying and bopping. His dance grew more and more sexual in nature. Twisting, turning his body, and arching his back rolling his stomach as his arms wound in intricate shapes. He caught sight of the people watching him, amongst them James. His eyes wide, reflecting the light of the party. Dean drew up close to James and rubbed his buttocks down his front. He turned his head so his eyes met James'.

"Would you like to join me?" he whispered.

It was James turn to be dumbstruck, as Dean grabbed hold of his hand and dragged him to the dance floor. Their bodies moved close to one another's, touching intimately. They gyrated their hips and thrust in perfect unison. Their bodies a melded, conjoined feast of pure sexual tension and desire. Minds as well as bodies were aflame, burning with barely pent up sexuality. As the music quickened so too did their movements till it was nothing more than a frenzy of twisting and turning upon each other. Their bodies never losing contact for one second during the whole dance. As the music wound down in its intensity so did their dance, their bodies slowing, their chest heaving, and their panting loud and exaggerated. The music stopped and Dean slumped onto James utterly exhausted, supported only by the other body. His hair stood on end as James' breath warmed the bare skin of his neck. He could feel the other boy's heart beating madly in his slim chest as Dean laid there in his arms.

"Oh my God," was the only words James could manage.

Dean smiled at the remark, he had made an impression of that he was sure, because he could feel the bulge that had begun to grow in James' jeans.

"I think I need a sit down and I think you need to compose yourself," Dean motioned downwards with his eyes smiling cheekily.

James just cleared his throat in embarrassment and walked with Dean away from the people and to the reclusion of the forests edge. They sat next to each other, their backs against a tree in complete silence for the rest of the night. Each too embarrassed to say anything to one another. They watching passively as the other people danced and started to leave. The numbers soon began to dwindle as more and more left the party. Dean looked at his watch; it was close to four in the morning. Dawn was but a few hours away and he knew his absence would have been discovered already. He looked up and saw the full moon still shining brightly. He turned to James, who had his head against the tree, his eyes closed. Dean thought how peaceful he looked. The pale light washing over him, making his features all the more handsome to Dean. He saw Mel walking over to him smiling widely. As she got to Dean he pressed a finger to his lips.

"Dean I'm going home now love, but I see you made quite an impression earlier," she whispered.

"Yeah so it would seem. But I might as well come with you and face the music. My folks are going to kill me," he said in hushed tones.

He rose to leave when he felt a hand grab him by the wrist. He turned to see James holding onto him, his eyes gleaming in the bright moonlight.

"Don't leave, not yet Dean please," he said almost pleadingly.

Dean looked at James and his heart melted due to the way he was looking at him. He turned to Mel and she seemed to understand his look all too well.

"Erm.........Well guys I'm out of here. I need some sleep, have fun you two," winking at Dean as she left.

They both said their goodbyes to Mel and Dean sat back down next to James. James let go of Dean's wrist and held his hand gently and with his other stroked Deans cheek lightly. Dean closed his eyes and let out a sigh. And then he felt lips touch his in a tentative kiss. His eyes shot open in surprise to see James leaning in close for a quick kiss. Dean followed through with a far more passionate snog, catching James by surprise. Dean ran his fingers through James' hair and held him by the back of the neck as they kissed each other with as much passion as they could. The kisses becoming harder as their bodies fell to the cold slightly damp ground. Leaves carpeting its surface, the sickly smell of damp surrounding them both and smoke rising from the few unlit fires. Crackles of burning wood from those still lit could be heard, casting a fitful light upon them.

Dean straddled James' stomach and continued kissing him. He could feel the bulge in his jeans again, growing larger and harder. James placed his hands on Dean's buttocks and clenched them roughly through his jeans. Dean pulled James' shirt up and ran his hands over his lean smooth stomach. They were too engrossed in each other's bodies to hear the rustling and cracking of twigs coming from the forest. Eyes were watching them from the darkness, large and yellow in colour and glinting in the moonlight as it filtered through the trees. Thick, slimy drool running from their jaws, their hunger and urge to hunt growing unbearable in the sight of the moon. They inched closer to the forests edge, growling to each other. A large black wolf padded its way through the others. It dwarfed his fellow wolves, the alpha male, his body a rippling mass of muscle. He watched the two boys touching and kissing with a morbid fascination. Like a hunter watching the animal frolicking through his gun sight before he pulls the trigger. His eyes gave the impression of a deep intelligence now lost.

Dean moved further down his body and unbuttoned James' jeans, pulled the zip down and exposed a pair of tight white underpants, straining to release its contents. Dean massaged the hard member, making James moan in pleasure. He pulled his underpants down, his hard penis flopping to full erection. Curved and full headed, Dean rubbed the tip with one finger, smearing the pre-come across its surface. James gave a small grunt. His arse wriggled in the soft, wet ground as Dean took a firm hold of his hard cock. Slowly rubbing the soft, smooth foreskin over the enlarged glands, it oozed more fluid as the pleasure grew. James groaned with his eyes closed.

The alpha male, pounced and came crashing through the trees. Breaking branches and twigs with his shear bulk. Soon the other wolves ran from their cover, darting off in different directions like a living wave of fur and muscle. Teeth bared and eyes filled with savage hunger for the hunt, snapping at the people ferociously in an almost rabid nature. Their human minds lost within the savagery of their wolf spirits. Pure werewolves, devoid of the human traits that force their change back to their human form, becoming totally trapped in their wolf bodies, slowly driven mad and consumed by base emotions. They charged with an evil intent, focused purely on satisfying their hunger to hunt. Eyes filled with hate as they leap atop people, bringing them down with savage efficiency. Ripping into them, tearing large chunks from them while the people still lived in a mad, blood crazed frenzy. The large alpha male stood in amongst the carnage, totally focused on Dean and James. Who now were pinned against the trunk of the tree in terror. Their faces twisted with the fear that coursed through their minds. Huddled together, grasping tight for as much safely as they could. The wolf padded closer to them, slowly. His gaze never leaving the two of them, the eyes taking on an uncomfortable softness, tempered by the slavering jaws that lay beneath. Something in the back of his mind was drawing him to these humans. A small vestige of his humanity that still remained though fractured and distant, he took another step closer and another.

Then the trance snapped, his mind reverting back to its wild state. He shot at Dean and James with almost unnatural speed. The wolf sunk his teeth into James' shoulder, who screamed in unbelievable agony. He was lifted up and thrown over the alpha wolves back. He landed awkwardly, breaking his right leg in several places and fracturing three ribs. His cries of pain were so loud startling even the werewolves as they fed. The alpha werewolf gave Dean a fearsome look then turned his back on him, slowly walking towards James. Who tried his best to get away, but even he knew it was impossible. As he tried to pick himself up the wolf put a large pad on his chest and pushed him back down. It put its full weight on James; the ribs cracked and broke under the creature's bulk. Puncturing his lungs in several places, he coughed up blood as his air ways filled with his own life fluid, slowly choking to death. The alpha wolf looked at James directly into his eyes, watching the life ebb out of him. And just before he died, the wolf ripped his throat out of his neck. Blood being flung all over his fur, forming a puddle around James' head like a disturbing halo.

He turned back to Dean, blood matting his snout and dripping onto the ground. Dean looked at the body of James over the wolves shoulder, horrified at the sight, his eyes wide and tears rolling down his cheeks, crying silently. The wolf saw this and cocked his head to one side, his eyes showing mild amusement. Though he knew not what he was amused at. He took another step closer menacingly. Dean shrunk back, pressing himself against the tree trying to put as much space between him and the wolves slavering jaws as he could. But even he knew a few inches wouldn't make any difference. The wolf shot at Dean; it took his left arm and dragged him along the ground, the canines slicing into the flesh, ripping the muscles. Dean tried to pull his arm away, but the tendons and sinew were ripped to pieces. Unable to move the now ravaged arm, he hit out at the wolf with his other hand, but with little effect. He tried to pull at the ears, but still this was no help. He was still dragged along the ground. Dean dug his fingers into the wolf's eye, the soft orb popping, and jelly like fluid spurting from the ruined eye. The wolf yipped in pain, let go of Dean's arm and jumped back. He growled in pain and anger. Dean tried to move away but the pain was preventing him. The wolf circled around his prone body, the purest anger showing in his one remaining eye. It grabbed Dean by his right hip and swung him with all his strength, Dean flew through the air, landing on the ground hard, his arm ripping and tearing further. Dean cried out, as blood began to flow from his arm and his hip where his flesh was missing. The milky white bone showing in amongst the bloody pulpy wound, Dean began to feel drowsier as he lost more of his blood.

The wolf strode over to Dean with purpose and intent. He stood over Dean and placed his paws on Dean's shoulders, holding him fast to the ground, unable to move. The wolf ripped at Dean left eye, the eye being pulled from the socket. The skin being ripped from his face and his cheek missing, the inside of his mouth and teeth clearly seen through the wound. Dean tried to cry out, but it came as nothing but a gurgle as blood filled his mouth. The pain was unbearable, he wished the wolf wound just kill him, anything for the pain to cease. Then he heard a loud, low howl from the distance. The wolf shot up, his ears pricked. He tested the air, he looked afraid. The wolf gave a growl to the other wolves. Who in turn stopped feeding from the many bodies that were around and ran back into the darkness off the forest, to its safety. The alpha wolf gave Dean another look then ran off himself. Dean tried to roll over, the earlier howl worrying him. Pain shot from his hip, causing him to once again cry out. He could see movement out of remaining eye though everything was blurred with the pain and adrenaline. But he could make out the basic shape of a canine like creature. It came towards him, slowly. Dean flopped back down and closed his eye. He knew his time had come; he was going to die this night. He felt the cold wet nose prod him, and a tongue lightly lick his skin, heard the soft padding of paws walking around him to the other side. Then he could feel soft fur on his right arm as the animal laid next to him. He began to skirt along the border of consciousness due to blood loss, his mind threatening to be cast into oblivion. But the dog made sure he remained awake with gentle prods of his nose and quiet whimpers.

Chapter 8

He awoke to a foggy and blurred world, every sound hushed and distant. His mind drifting, unable to focus on the objects around him but his sense of smell was overpowering, the scent of cleaning fluids and blood lingered in the air. Surrounding him and penetrating his very skin with its foulness. He couldn't feel his arm; he tried to turn his head to look at it. But pain shot through his neck and face, causing his mind to swim and his vision blur. He felt someone place their hand on his head, soothing the heat and pain with their cool skin. He opened his eye to see who it was. But there was nobody there, and he could see no people outside the curtains. As far as he knew he was alone, however he didn't feel alone. He still felt drowsy, and still lingered on the edge of consciousness. Slipping into the darkness his mind was filled with strange and wild scenes. He dreamt of dark, forgotten forests, moonlit lakes and breath-taking mountains. Wilderness like he has never seen before, but it didn't feel like a dream. More like a memory, but it wasn't his. The images soon faded into oblivion.

The morning sun filtered through the gaps in the Venetian blinds. Casting strips of light across the room. The smell still remained but he had soon become accustomed to it, but every now and then he got a small hint of a scent he seemed to recognise but couldn't place. He could feel a slight tingling in his left arm at the elbow, and in the left side of his face. It was like an itch he couldn't scratch, annoying him day and night. And the sensation was getting stronger with each passing hour.

Once again he felt the reassuring touch on his forehead, soothing his tension and fear. As he opened his eyes he saw that he was alone, as he was the last time. It was scaring him, was he going mad, and was he already insane. He didn't know but all he knew was this feeling that he wasn't totally alone. Like the feeling you get when someone is watching you, but this was far stronger. He heard movement from the other side of the door, but he heard it clearly. Not muffled like it should have been, it was like the noise was coming from inside the room. He strained to move his neck in order to look at the door, it hurt but it wasn't as bad as it was. He had obviously been given a hefty dose of painkillers. He squinted with his good eye trying to see through the semi clear curtains surrounding his bed. As the door opened, light flooded the shaded room stinging Deans eye causing him to close it quickly and turn his head away.

He heard the door close, the sound of the latch clicking into place hurting his ears slightly. He didn't understand why all the sounds were so loud and painful to him. He turned his head to see who had come into his room. It was his father; his expression was that of horror. It was then he realised just how serious his injuries were. He felt a single tear well up it his eye, slowly running down his cheek and making a small inconsequential spot on the pillow case. However in that single tear was contained all his pain, his fear and sorrow. His eye soon started to well with more and more tears, all rolling to join the first, making the dot of damp grow. He could see the redness in his Fathers eyes; it was obvious he had been sobbing, his cheeks still damp from his tears. He reached out his right arm to his father, who grabbed his hand with both of his and held it tight. With that his father broke down, dropping to a squat in fits of despair, tears flooding his eyes. Dean knew why he was crying. It was obvious. He wouldn't survive this, his injuries were too bad. Dean opened his mouth to talk but found he couldn't. His face was too badly mangled. But something in his eye must have conveyed what he wanted to say, because his father responded.

"Dean you have nothing to be sorry for, you didn't know this was going to happen," his father said, his voice cracking slightly at the end.

Dean nodded his head, letting his dad know he understood. He looked around the room for his mother, but she wasn't there. Where was she, why wasn't she here with him while he was laid dying. Then he heard her, a loud wailing sob from the corridor. She must have been inconsolable. He could hear a man telling her he was sorry but there was nothing more he could do but make him comfortable. It was the doctor telling her their only child was as good as dead. The noise his mother was making was unbearable. Utterly horrible to listen to, such was her pain and desperation. He tried to shut it out, tried to listen to anything else he could. But nothing would drown out his mother's cries of anguish. He felt himself flirt on the edge of consciousness, the blackness coming to take him. Pulling himself away from it, he feared if he should drop into unconsciousness he may never again awake. No he must fight it, for his mother he must fight. He opened his eye wearily to see his father still on the floor sobbing. Dean squeezed his father's hand more tightly. Who seemed to understand and stood to leave, giving his son a fierce squeeze of the hand. Dean turned his head towards the window in order to shield his sensitive eye from the invading unnatural light. There was a very slight breeze coming in through the vents, carrying with it a plethora of smells and scents. Dean sense of smell was as though it had awoken from a long slumber. It was amazing; he could smell every intricacy of the night air. The animals searching for food in the dumpsters and the heavy perfume of women as they walked past his window. The stinking fumes from passing vehicles. He was sniffing away with almost impatience, as though he had to smell everything as soon as he could. It was as though he had become an animal, turning primal.

He was sniffing with his eye closed when he heard the door open again. Turning he could see a white coat through the thin curtains, he knew who it was. Every part of his body was dreading what the doctor had to say. It was sure to be bad, after the way his father and mother had reacted. As the doctor made his way through the curtains his features became clear. He knew instantly from the man's demeanour there was no hope. He was going to die. The doctor pulled up a chair and sat down. He placed a hand gently and sensitively on Dean's shoulder, it was obvious from his face he didn't look forward to the task that lay before him.

"Dean, your wounds are grave indeed and though we could stop the bleeding with surgery. You have lost a great deal of blood and no matter how much we seem to give you it doesn't make any difference. It's as though your body is rejecting the donor blood even though it's a perfect match. We all agree if we did operate you wouldn't survive. All we can do is make you comfortable and await the inevitable. I'm so sorry," he said leaning forward keeping his tone soft and comforting.

It didn't matter to Dean if he was sorry or not, he had just told him he was dying. He hated him; he hated Mel for dragging him there in the first place. He hated the wolf for doing this to him. But the person he mostly hated was himself. It was he who caused all this pain and anguish, all because he accept his father telling him no. If only he hadn't been so concerned with climbing the social ladder at school he would be in his own bed, struggling to drag himself out for work. Not in a hospital on his death bed. He was an idiot. His heart fluttered in his chest slightly, as though it had skipped a beat. Then it started to beat heavily, growing stronger and stronger with each beat. The blood rushing through his veins until he could hear it in his ears pumping loudly, then came the pain from his wounds, causing him to moan. The doctor eyed him concerned. The pain was building, cascading in an ever increasing motion. He tried to scream but all that came out was another gurgle as blood filled his mouth again. He trashed around in his bed as the pain continued to get worse. The doctor ran for the emergency buzzer, its sound filling the room and Deans ears. He heard shouting from outside but in the haze of pain he couldn't understand them. The door swung open and with a flurry of motion a gaggle of doctors and nurses ran in. He was beginning to burn up, like he was on fire. He thrashed about in bed as the nurses tried to restrain him. But they couldn't he was too strong, he threw himself to the floor. Crashing to the hard surface, his mind so consumed with agony it proved unable to register how he got there. Every nerve in his body was ablaze with white hot pain, his moans growing louder as he thrashed with more strength. The nurses were grappling with him on their knees trying to keep him still so he didn't hurt himself further. He pulled some off their knees, sending them sprawling to the floor. The pain was getting worse and worse. Dean couldn't take it any longer; he just wanted it to stop. He closed his eye tightly as his body convulsed again. His flailing legs taking a doctor off his feet, smashing into the wall as he fell. Just when he thought he couldn't take anymore, his eye shot open and he let out a very loud throaty growl that reverberated within his chest. As he dropped back in an exhausted heap he fell into unconsciousness. Once again in he was in a dark forest, the bright full moon giving the world a bluish grey hue. He was running through the undergrowth, splashing in small streams and howling at the moon. Continuing to play and cavort amongst the majestic trees till he got laid down on a soft patch of grass and fell into a deep and restful sleep.

He awoke to be greeted by the sweet smell of dawn wafting through his window, the soft dew on the grass, the sour dampness of the soil. He heard birds ushering in the new day from miles away. He looked around the shaded room as if he was seeing it for the first time. He felt like a new man, strong and in control. The warming light coming from behind the blinds was a welcome alternative to the previous night. As he sat himself up in bed the image of the forest was still in his mind, slowly fading away till it was nothing but a ghostly negative in his memory. He blinked in the bright morning sun, feeling a tingle from his other eye. Like the lashes lightly stroking the bandage. But he knew that was impossible, the wolf left nothing there. He lifted his hand to his face and felt at the bandage and to his surprise he felt flesh underneath. Not just bone as it had last night. He didn't understand what was happening, but he did understand it wasn't normal. It wasn't human. He felt around his head, looking for the end of the bandage, he undid it and started to unravel. As he got to the last few layers he could see the light coming through the thin material. He didn't know how it was possible to lose an eye and then for it to return within one night. He continued unwrapping his dressings and dropped the balled up bandages on the floor beside his bed. Gingerly touching his face, feeling the firm, smooth skin where previously there hadn't been any. Shock causing him to laugh loudly as he blinked a few times, the sensation new and alien to his eye, his sight was a little blurred but he could see at least. He looked down at his arm, and tried to flex his fingers. To his amazement they moved, the muscles and digits were tight and felt weak but at least they moved. He tried to move his elbow; it was so tight it moved with an audible creak that caused him a great deal of pain. The discomfort soon began to lift as the joint was exercised though. He ripped away the bandages with haste, it was all healed the skin was just a little red and raw. It was newly grown skin, he stroked it lightly feeling the short thin hairs that had begun to grow on its surface. He was in shock he couldn't believe it. Feeling his hip he soon realised that too was fully healed. Slowly peeling back the bloody dressing to reveal smooth, soft skin untouched by any blemish, he shook his head in amazement.

For what seemed a lifetime he just sat there and stared at the newly grown flesh, unable to think of anything but the fact it was impossible. Then suddenly it was as if he was knocked out of a trance. He jumped out of bed, running over to the window and pulled up the blinds basking in the beautifully warm dawn sunlight. Its rays like a new experience on his brand new skin. Tingling and causing goose bumps to pop up across its surface. He closed his eyes and listened to the world beyond the glass, he could hear people talking as thought they were in the same room, radios in passing cars as though it was his radio. He raised his nose to the vent and sniffed. Almost being knocked to the floor by the sensation of smells assaulting his olfactory glands, the strong perfume of flowers, and the noxious scent of nearby factories. Both as beguiling as the other, all new and strange to him, never had the world taken on this amount of dimension or colour. It was like seeing the world for the first time with news eyes. To explain it in detail would be like trying to explain colour to a creature with no eyes. It was simply impossible to explain it to someone else. The world seemed more beautiful to him. He leant forward with his hands on the window sill and laughed in total relief and shock.

He heard movement from outside of his door, as he turned the door opened. In walked a man, although he had platinum hair he didn't look a year over forty five. Casting Dean a warm smile he walked across the room, looking him over. His soft and comforting eyes settled upon Deans own and bore into his soul. Searching for something, till he blinked and his smile grew warmer. He gave a small nod and perched himself on the edge of the hospital bed. Dean had never seen this man before, but he felt as though he knew him in the most intimate of ways, almost like they were kin, children of the same mother. His smile remained warm and affectionate as Dean watched him for what felt like an age. He searched the pale slate eyes for any information on why he felt like he knew him. His slim noble aquiline face bore no resemblance to anyone he knew or had known.

"I know you, but yet I have never met you in my life," Dean remarked his tone on of utter confusion.

"Oh we met the other night youngster. You were in a bad way, I'm surprised you survived," the older man said, "But look at you now, fully healed and in only a few short hours. Faster than I thought possible, how very unusual."

"I don't understand are you one of the paramedics," Dean's confusion grew.

The man laughed, a soft and friendly sound, he was obviously amused by the whole situation.

"No I'm no paramedic, I'm Alexius. We did meet the night of the attack, but long before any humans found you. Can you not

72

remember the touch of my fur against your skin, the sound of my whimpers as I tried to comfort you?"

Dean began to become worried, scared this person was insane. Or perhaps it was he that had gone mad, his mind trapped within his dying body. Then his memories drifted back to that night and remembered the dog that had lain next to him. But he was sure that wasn't possible, he hoped that wasn't possible. Slowly he backed off, towards the wall.

Alexius' smile dropped and his eyes grew sad, "You really don't know do you?"

"I haven't got a clue what you're talking about!" Dean replied quickly.

"Look kid I'm sorry, really I am," he took in a deep breath before releasing it in a heavy sigh, "You were bitten, bitten by a pure werewolf during a full moon. These creatures aren't like the rest of our kin, they're savage. Driven mad by the beast inside us all, they can never again take on human form, living for the hunt and only for the hunt."

"You're a madman! Fucking insane! Get out!" Dean shouted his heart beating madly in his chest.

Alexius nodded his head, seeming to understand, "Denial is totally natural. However remember what happened to you, remember the way the wolves acted. Think about how your life threatening wounds healed over a matter of hours. Then tell me I'm mad afterwards."

Dean did as Alexis had told him. He looked inside himself and realised he felt it was true. He remembered that night, and realised how many of the wolves mannerisms were human like. About how the big one that attacked Dean looked at him and James. The way his eyes showed emotion unlike that of any normal animal and how he reacted when he gouged out his eye, almost like revenge. Dean took his eye so the wolf would repay him in kind. He didn't want to believe it but Alexis was right. It was the only explanation that could be used to explain it all. He was attacked by a werewolf, and he had now become a werewolf. The realisation was like a heavy weight on his shoulders, forcing him to drop to the floor. His heart filled with sorrow, he looked up at Alexis and began to cry.

"I'm a monster, I'm a fucking monster. A werewolf!" shouted Dean, "why did this happen to me! Why?!"

"Dean you're not a monster, think about how you felt stood at the window. The beauty of this world, the freedom you felt. Beauty only a werewolf could see and freedom only an immortal could feel. This isn't a curse, it's a blessing. .

Alexius helped Dean to his feet with great ease, his warm smile reinforcing his sincere words. He laid a hand on Dean's slender shoulder and gave it a heartfelt squeeze before heading for the door. As he opened it he turned back to Dean.

"Look after yourself young one, people will not treat you the way they did if they knew the truth. Humans fear what they don't understand and usually destroy what they fear. I know you wish to see your family, but remember they think you should be dead, they will shun you, they will fear what you represent. But I know you will still go," he smiled, "We all do. If you ever need me, use your nose, you will be able to find me."

As Alexis left Dean turned back to the window, he looked out at the world, a world that had changed for him now. Everything was different. He was different. The world had taken on a brand new splendour, he needed to get out and see it. Bask in it. But first he needed some clothes. He went to the door and eased it open; popping his head out looking if anybody was around. The coast was clear, he was safe for now. He snuck out of his room and crept along the corridor till he got to the laundry. Grabbing some medical scrubs he quickly put them on his naked body, chaffing his new flesh as the rough material slid over it. When he grabbed the handle he heard someone walking down the corridor. Their shoes clicking on the hard surface, Dean pressed himself against the wall. His heart started to beat heavily like it did the other night as the clicking stopped outside the door. He was going to be discovered. He knew he was. Then to his relief the person kept moving further down the corridor. This was his chance but he had to be quick.

He burst out through the door, crashing into the opposite wall jarring his shoulder. The nurses must have heard the commotion as they soon came running down the corridor after him. He had no idea how he was going to escape now, the exit was past them. He could smell the outside from the air coming through the doors. He ran away from them as fast as his legs could carry him, but being no longer human that was faster than Dean anticipated, arriving at the end of the corridor in just a matter of seconds.

"Way COOL!" he exclaimed.

He could hear the sounds of the nurse's footfalls echoing down the corridor as they ran after him. Eagerly looking left and right for an escape route, but he found none, even the windows wouldn't open enough to climb out. His only chance was in the opposite direction past his pursuers. Whatever he was going to do he had to be quick, he could hear them drawing closer. So he pressed his back against the wall, closed his eyes and hoped with his new speed he could barge past them. Pushing himself from the wall he sprinted towards the oncoming people, opening his eyes just in time to see the nurses round the corner. His legs carried him with supernatural ease as he pumped the muscles harder. Drawing closer and without thinking, acting on pure natural instinct he leapt into the air sailing over their heads landing in a forward roll. Immediately carrying on running before the nurses had even turned around, he ran through the hospital like a man on a mission, when he got to the automatic doors he stopped running and casually walked out. Taking a lung full of fresh air and exhaling loudly. He shook himself free of the shackles of human life and was ready to fully embrace his new life. Looking up at the bright sun he smiled at the welcoming warmth on his face. The world was ready for him and he felt ready for it. He walked off into the light warm summer breeze.

Chapter 9

He stood at the corner of the street and cautiously looked at the house. Unsure whether he should go or not, Alexius' words worried him. Would his family accept him. Would they treat him like the Dean they knew, the Dean they loved. Or like a freak. He didn't know but they were his family. They deserved this chance to see him, for good or ill. However he hoped they could accept him, but he didn't know how they would react. After all he wasn't human anymore.

Walking the short distance to the front of his house he was unsure if he should either walk straight in or knock. So he loitered at the bottom of the stairs, his nervousness clear from his body language. He spun round quickly deciding on his course of action when the door opened. His father was just walking out, obviously going to visit him from the flowers in his hands. Their smell wafted towards Dean who inhaled deeply, savouring the sweet, pleasant scent. A smile spread across his face, they were tulips his favourite. Looking up warmly at his father, who instead of being happy was shocked, even afraid. Tears formed at the corners of Deans eyes, he knew then Alexius had been right this was a grave mistake. His father dropped the bunch of flowers and shook his head in disbelief. As Dean started to walk up the steps, his father retreated backwards into the house. He held out his hand to his father, who swatted it away like a dirty, germ carrying bug. He slammed the door shut. Dean leapt up the last few steps and began to bang on the door.

"Dad let me in, it's me Dean, please I beg you don't do this," he pleaded.

"Get away you should be dead, you're not my son, leave us alone!" his father shouted from the other side of the door.

Dean sobbed as he banged on the door repeatedly, his blows growing heavier. He heard the wood of the door creak as it began to split. His pleading took on a more beast like sound, almost like a growl as he hammered on the door. The wood finally gave way, his fist going through the door gouging deep furrows in the flesh of his hand. He saw his father's horrified face through the hole he had made. True he may not be a monster, but even he knew he was acting like one. His head dropped in shame.

"I'm sorry..............Bye," he murmured.

He trudged down the stairs, his steps heavy with sorrow. He had been reborn into a new and exciting world. And now he was alone, no family and no friends. Then he remembered what Alexius said about following his nose.

So he did, he closed his eyes and sniffed the air. Something at the back of his mind was telling him to head towards the forest. His keen senses and his wolfen instincts guiding him through the multitude of scents, he sniffed as he walked, following the scent that his mind had latched onto. Soon drawing closer to the source he stood at the edge of the forest. The place he never wanted to enter ever again but yet almost being urged to step over the threshold. His mind filled with memories from the night his life changed forever. He shook the images from his mind, his features becoming etched with a steely determination. Alexius was his only hope. He didn't fully understand everything yet; he seemed to be acting of reflex mostly. The only way he could learn to use his new abilities was for another werewolf to teach him, even one a few days old like himself knew that. He needed a mentor and Alexius was the only other of his kind he knew. He followed the trail of scent, over logs and around small lakes and across shallow streams. Soon a small log cabin came into view, smoke rising from its chimney. A light was burning inside as he stepped onto the porch. As he reached up to knock on the door, it opened. Alexis was there smiling, he tapped the side of his nose.

"I smelt you when you got to the forest," he said smiling.

"I need hel......................" was all Dean could manage before he burst into tears.

"You went to see your family didn't you?" he didn't need an answer but instead gestured for him to enter, "We all do, even when we know it's pointless."

Dean dropped onto the sofa, his shoulders heavy and weary, tears still running down his cheeks. Alexis sat next to him, and put an arm round him. He tried to comfort him the best he could, but he knew he would have to deal with it himself. It's a big thing to no longer be human and be alone in the world. Everything you once knew, crumbling into dust and becoming nothing but ties to a life that had been lost. He nodded as Dean opened his heart to him, telling him about his fears. It was all he could do.

Dean soon stopped crying, his tears spent and his eyes red. He tried to smile. But all he could manage was a weak half smile.

"I'm sorry, really I should be happy. I was dying a few hours ago and now I'm not, but………." he trailed off unsure how to explain his warring emotions.

"You lost everything you have even known, even your humanity, I understand," a warm smile spreading across his face, "So what's your name?"

"It's Dean, Dean Johnson."

Alexius squeezed Dean's shoulder a little before standing and looking out of the window. Dean relaxed a little and sat back in the sofa. He cast his gaze around the room; a large open fire dominated the far wall. Heat could still be felt coming from it even though it was now out. Wispy trails of smoke came from the glowing embers left in the grate. A couple of leather sofas were placed around a bare wooden coffee table which had a worn rug beneath it. The whole place had a rustic quality about it. Dean guessed a kitchen, bathroom and bedroom would be found through the single door situated in the opposite wall. As he surveyed the room his mind drifted to his own future. To all intents and purposes he was homeless. He had lost everything and had nowhere to go. Looking at Alexius who was stood at the window gazing at the surrounding forest, Dean hoped he would help yet again.

"Alexius, could I possibly stop for a little while, just till I get myself sorted," his voice asked but his eyes pleaded, "I've got nowhere to go."

"Of course, you may stop as long as you like," he smiled widely and invitingly, "Mi casa as tu casa."

"Thanks for everything," Dean said sincerely.

Alexis merely winked in way of your welcome, and turned back to the window. The sun was just filtering through the canopy, casting fit full shadows across the ground as the breeze moved the branches. Dean looked out of the other window, the forest looked so inviting. More so than it did when he was human, almost like it was beckoning him, pleading with him to come out and walk through its trees. Play in its rivers and lakes. Just to enjoy himself. He looked over at Alexis who had been watching him. He smiled and cocked his head towards the forest. Dean just nodded his head, knowing what he was asking. They both left the cabin, the forest their true habitat.

Chapter 10

Dean awoke to be greeted by the bright morning sun shining through his bedroom window, the sizzle of fat and the mouth-watering smell of frying bacon. He inhaled deeply, stretched out his body ridding his muscles from the weariness induced by a restful night, smiling when he heard joyous and contented whistling coming from the kitchen. Springing from his bed in one movement he pulled on some baggy jeans and an old jumper before heading for the door. As he opened his door he was confronted by a tangible wall of scent so strong it almost knocked him to his knees. Even though he had been with Alexius for three years he still hadn't got the hang of controlling his senses yet. But he was learning and he had been taught much in that time. Shaking his head when he heard a particularly bum note from Alexius as he stalked into the kitchen and sat on the edge of the table.

"You know, you could be making yourself useful like setting the table or something," Alexius said without turning his head. But Dean knew he would be smiling.

Dean cursed his mentor's senses silently; he had been trying to creep up on him for ages but could never manage it. He would always know he was there. Dean crossed the kitchen and started to collect up the plates and cutlery they would need. As he crossed back towards the table, he peeked over Alexius' shoulder at his breakfast frying. The bacon was well done and crisp, his mouth salivated causing him to lick his lips in anticipation. A werewolf was perpetually hungry, their metabolism so fast they required four times as much food as an average human. Alexis nudged him with his elbow; he smiled as the cook cracked a couple of eggs into the spitting bacon fat. Dean had just finished setting the table when Alexius turned with the still bubbling frying pan. He placed seven rashers of bacon and a fried egg on each plate. As he put the frying pan back on the stove the toaster popped up with four slices off toast. Picking them up he ended up throwing them at Dean as they burnt his fingers. Dean started laughing as he caught them. Alexius gave him a look that just made Dean laugh harder. As he sat at the table Dean had already started to eat furiously, his apatite had grown immensely. Alexius just chuckled at him; Dean thought that he had missed the company. From what he could gather he'd been alone for a while. He didn't like to pry into his past, though Alexius didn't seem to mind talking about it. In fact he seemed to enjoy talking about the past with a fellow werewolf, someone who would understand him or wouldn't judge him. He had grown to depend upon him for his tutoring and Alexius likewise seemed to depend upon him to keep him sane. It was the first night of the lunar cycle tonight; Dean was looking forward to it. He had sort of got used to the pain, he just had to learn to relax then it would begin to hurt less, still so much to learn about his new life.

While Dean ate in haste, Alexius took his time chewing his food. He eyed Dean and smiled. He had missed the company of a fellow werewolf. It was relaxing and uplifting to see one with so much energy and enthusiasm. Someone who grabs their destiny with both hands unflinchingly. Alexius could see this boy was something more than a mere werewolf, he would become something great. And his personality was to his liking also, fun, cheeky and clearly loving. He enjoyed his time with Dean, it was fun. That wasn't a thing he had experienced for a while. Humans couldn't understand a werewolf's humour; they were still constrained by decorum as well as mortality. A werewolf just couldn't take life seriously anymore, they were free. Free from death, old age and societies pressure to conform to the ideal. He was surprised at how quickly Dean had taken to his immortal life though; it was as though he had been born this way.

Dean shovelled the last of his bacon in to his mouth, his jaw straining to chew it. Alexius just shook his head at him, Dean smiled back with a cheeky grin. He reminded Alexius of a cheeky little school kid that could flutter his eyelashes, smile and get away with murder. Alexius lent back on his chair, filled with thoughts and memories, memories of times past.

As Alexius was reminiscing, Dean was itching to get out into the forest, urging the sun to set, almost willing it. It was the way with young werewolves, highly strung when the lunar cycle was close. Their energy and excitement growing, but tempered with worry of the pain that was to come. Dean had never gotten used to it, but it had lessened over the years. His legs were shaking from the excitement;

he felt a bare foot land on his knee stopping his leg from moving. As he looked down he saw it was Alexius', it was clawed and had long hairs growing from it. He'd always envied his ability to partially change at will. He eyed Alexius with narrowed eyes, but a little twinkle in one corner betraying his true emotion. Alexius saw this and smiled. Dean loved him, he had become a father to the young werewolf. He was there for him when nobody else was. And if he was honest he felt for like a son, someone who needed his love as well as his tutoring. Fate had brought them together, but Alexius had a feeling it was something more than mere fate. He placed the last piece of bacon in his mouth and chewed it slowly. It was maybe noon at the latest he judged from the light that shone through the windows. It would be around ten hours till the change called to them, and once again they would be able to let the beast loose. Just for those three nights, this was how werewolves controlled their inner animal. By letting it out for a while, like taking a dog for a walk. He could feel Dean's leg vibrating the table again as it shook with almost uncontrollable energy.

"Dean, calm down will you. You're like a bitch on heat," Alexius said without looking at him.

"Sorry," he mumbled.

Dean rose from the table and placed his plate in the sink before leaving the kitchen. He wanted a walk to clear his head, he was getting too anxious. As he left the cabin he felt better, like a wave of calmness had washed over him. He inhaled the forest air, feeling the tingle of pollen at the back of his nose. A smile crept along his face as he exhaled. He loved the smell of spring; he closed his eyes and listened to the sweet music of life, the birds singing their chirpy little songs, the rodents rustling in the undergrowth and deer grazing among the few clearings that could sustain wild grass, the male's antlers clashing for their right to mate with the females. All these made life seem more beautiful and precious than he had previously thought possible. He had always liked nature but now it was far much more, it was his home, welcoming him back every time he stepped out. He started to walk into the woods; he knew it would be hours before the start of his turning but it just made him feel better walking in these woods. Calmed his soul and relaxed his anxiousness. He started to think about all the things he had learnt from Alexius, the rules and the tricks he had gathered over his years as a werewolf. The only way you can become that knowledgeable is by experience. After all when you are bitten it doesn't come with a guide book. As he walked he met people who were hiking along the paths, he smiled warmly and gave them greeting. But Alexius had warned him to never get too deeply involved with humans. If they could kill one of their own kind, imagine what they would do to us he used to always say. Dean thought it was a pessimistic way of looking at humans, but he could understand the reasons for it. He just had to look at his own experiences with humans, namely his own family. They do tend to fear what they don't understand and mostly try to destroy what they fear.

"Hi," he heard someone say in front of him.

He looked at the person who was stood in front of him. It was a young man, maybe nineteen but he looked a lot younger. His smile caused cute dimples in his cheeks and his large brown eyes twinkled in the bright sunlight. Brown hair, cut short and spiked swayed in the breeze like soft dark grass. He blinked a couple of times, his eye lashes fluttering. Dean's senses were flooded with the scent and pheromones coming from the person. Dean picked up a heightened sexuality; the boy was attracted to him. Dean smiled back.

"Hi right back at you," he said.

This made the guy giggle slightly. Dean couldn't believe it; he was flirting with this guy. He was so usually shy and reserved but not now it would seem. As he drew closer his scent got stronger, driving Dean almost wild with lust. It was his dormant animal side that was beginning to awaken. Urging him to mount the lad, Dean fought against the urges till they subsided a little. Dean offered a hand to the guy who took it and shook it gently. His hands soft and warm in Deans grip. He could feel the guys pulse, it was heavy and fast. Dean smile broadened, showing his white teeth, stark against the redness of his full lips.

"You seemed in your own little world there," the lad said.

"Yeah I was, but I've just come back to earth with a bump," Dean said smiling.

This made the guy giggle even more, the light dancing in his eyes. Dean had not felt like this since he was with James. The name making his heart hurt, it was still a horrible and traumatic memory for him. He would have nightmares about the attack from time to time. But he pushed the memory to the back of his mind. He felt a hand touch his bare forearm gingerly.

"Would you care to walk with me," the guy said.

"I'd love to, my names Dean by the way," he said.

"Hi Dean I'm Peter, I live in town. I've never seen you there, are you local?" Peter asked.

"Well I live on the outskirts of town, in the forest actually," Dean said.

"Neat!" Peter said grabbing Dean's arm and holding it tightly.

Dean placed his free hand on Peters hand and felt comfortable. Once again he remembered the way he felt with James; he shook the thought from his mind. As they walked along the path into town, Peter drew closer and closer to Dean. Wrapping his arm round Deans. As they walked Dean talked to the other lad, Peter listened intently with his head resting on Deans shoulder. Seemingly happy to hear what he had to say, chipping in only a few times himself. As they traipsed through the forest, holding hands and talking they passed other people. Some smiled warmly, some giggled and others stared. But they didn't seem to notice them; they were too wrapped up in their own world. A world where Dean talked and Peter giggled. Dean was enjoying the walk; he knew Alexius wouldn't approve of it. Minimum contact with humans that's what he'd say, but what is a walk in the forest going to hurt. And besides why couldn't he have a relationship with someone, it had been three years after all. Peter seemed harmless enough he thought; he kissed him lightly on the top of the head. Peter stopped walking and looked at Dean, his eye wide in shock but a little grin on his face. Dean lent in closer and kissed him gingerly on the lips. When Peter reciprocated Dean kissed him more passionately. Their tongues flicking and caressing each other's, Dean lifted Peter of the floor who threw his legs round Dean's waist locking his feet together. Dean knew it was his animal side but he was so full of lust that he couldn't stop it. He lent Peter against a tree and ground his groin against Peters groin hard. Becoming more and more animalistic, he realised he was going to end up having sex right here right now if he didn't stop. So he pulled himself away from the kiss and fought back the lust that burnt inside him. Peter breathed heavily, his heart pounding in his chest. He dropped his legs from Dean and stood, still having to use the tree for support.

"WOW! You certainly know how to surprise a guy Dean, that was intense," Peter gasped out in between breaths.

"I'm sorry, I got a little carried away," Dean apologised.

"No don't be sorry it was fantastic, just didn't expect it that's all," said Peter his breath calmer.

He pulled Dean close, wrapping his arms round his waist laying his hands on Dean's tight buns. Dean smiled as he felt them rub on his skin. Peter lent in and gave him a passionate kiss, their lips locking for what seemed a life time. As they broke to take in air, Peter kissed Dean again this time lightly. They both hugged, their heads lent on each other's shoulders. Like they had been searching for each other their entire life and just this moment found each other. Dean remembered Alexius' words, but he couldn't be alone. Not for his whole life, the three years he had been with Alexius had almost killed him. Apart from his mentor he had nobody. He felt alone most of the time, only his sheer force of personality stopped him from going mad. Alexius was great as a friend and a tutor, but he wanted so much more than that. He hoped Peter could provide that, he hoped he would. He was so deep in thought he jumped when he felt Peter lick the end of his nose. When he opened his eyes Peter was smiling and giggling.

"You'd gone into your own little world again, so I thought that would be the best way of waking you up," Peter said giggling.

"Well yeah it did seem to work, you can wake me up like that every morning if you want," Dean said smiling.

"What..............Do you mean.................," Peter couldn't even ask the question.

"Peter would you like to go out with me?" Dean asked instead.

All Peter could do was nod slowly; his eyes wide open in shock. He threw his arms round Dean again, holding on tightly, almost fearing to let go in case he lost him. Dean also hugged him, pulling him closer till their bodies were pressed together tightly. Dean could feel Peter's heart pumping in his chest, it was beating heavily. Like he had just run a great distance, Dean knew it was the emotion that he felt because Dean felt the same. It was like finding a great treasure that you had searched a lifetime for. It was exhilarating, but also calming at the same time. Like a lifetime of work has finally come to an end and you can finally relax. The sun washed over them, mottled through the trees, the little spots of light warming their skin. Like the sun was casting a spotlight on their budding relationship. They basked in the bright warmth and their new found happiness.

They walked for what seemed like hours. Just walked and talked to each other. About nothing important, just simple likes and dislikes. Getting to know each other that little bit better, always walking hand in hand, Peter's head lent on Dean's strong shoulder. When Dean looked at the sky, the sun had dropped low. It was setting, soon it would be night. He closed his eyes preparing himself for his anxiousness. But it never came; he was still calm and relaxed. He felt Peter grasp his hand more tightly. Dean could feel the lads arm tense up and smell the fear in his scent. He opened his eyes to find they were no longer alone. Three other people were stood in front of them. Their shadows elongated by the dipping sun, casting Dean and Peter in shade. Their faces were stern; Dean could smell the anger coming from every pore that covered their bodies. He knew there was going to be a confrontation. His every muscle tensed in his body, preparing for a fight. The first of the people walked forward, his face a grimace. His blonde hair shaved extremely short, brown eyes narrowed in hatred. His lips curled in a cruel and mocking smile. The crooked nose just emphasised his fierceness. But Dean wasn't worried; he had become accustomed to his new found abilities. If he was pushed into it he could rip this man in two. The man took a step forward, his eyes turning cold. His other two friends also stepped forward to back him up. Dean merely smiled, it didn't matter if it was ten men, they still didn't stand a chance. The man with blonde hair whispered to his friends. They started to laugh.

"So you're a couple of queers then?" the man asked mockingly.

"Yeah we're gay.............and what's it got to do with you?" Dean spat out with distain.

The remark shocked the man slightly. But the shock soon turned to anger.

"This little queers got a mouth on him," the man said before unzipping his fly, "Grab him, lets show him how a homo is supposed to use their mouth."

His two friends moved towards Dean, who just pulled Peter behind him, out of the danger zone. He put his hands to the side with them open, trying not to show any aggression. He didn't want to fight, not with Peter here. But they didn't seem to care. So Dean motioned for Peter to back off. He did, his face etched with worry. Dean could smell the guy's pheromones, their sweat that clung to their underarm hair. They were strong compared to other humans but they were nowhere near the prowess of a werewolf. Dean punched the first man in the chest and felt the breast bone crack under his fist. It stopped the man in his tracks and clutched at the place Dean punched. The other man slowed in his charge, but it was too late Dean wouldn't stop now. He grabbed the man by his wrist and spun till the man was forced to the ground and screamed in pain. Dean twisted the arm more popping the joint out of its socket. His screams were deafening.

Dean turned to the man with blonde hair, dropped his head and narrowed his eyes before growling deep and menacingly. A challenge, but he didn't take it; instead he turned and ran in the opposite direction. Dean huffed in disgust.

He heard Peter gasp in amazement from behind him. Dean hoped he hadn't shown too much of his strength, it was easy to get carried away during the lunar cycle. He beckoned Peter closer. Peter cautiously walked towards Dean, but when Dean smiled at him warmly he could see there was nothing to worry about. He threw his arms round Dean's waist and sobbed heavily. Not through sadness or fear but through relief. Dean stroked at Peters hair trying to comfort him as best he could, his sobs came more slowly as he calmed down. Peter's knees gave way; Dean held him up and pulled him to his feet so their faces were level. Dean wiped away the tears with his thumb and smiled. He kissed Peter on the nose making him giggle a little as his lips tickled the tip of his nose. The sun was setting, growing a little darker. Dean knew he had to cut this short and get back to the cabin before the turn. He kissed Peter lovingly on the lips, while ever so softly stroking his cheek.

"I've got to go Peter, I must head home now," Dean said quietly.

"Will I see you again?" Peter asked.

"Oh you most certainly will, don't worry about that," Dean smiled.

Peter's eyes sparkled and glistened, wide like an innocent child, he pulled Dean closer in his arms, kissing him lightly on the lips. Dean finally felt that all was right with his life, he had adjusted to his new body, he was happy and now he had a boyfriend. Things seemed to be clicking into place for him. The sun was dipping low, he had to leave now. He said a hurried goodbye to Peter, parting with a kiss and a vow to see him again. Dean ran into the darkening forest as fast as he dared move with witnesses, his nose leading back to their hideaway. As he came into view of the wooden lodge he saw Alexius pacing up and down on the porch. Even from this distance he could see he was not happy. He ran up the slight incline towards the lodge, Alexius turned and saw him. His eyes narrowed, his jaw muscles tensed. Dean knew he was in for it, but at least it would be a short rant the change would soon be upon them.

"Where the hell have you been?!" Alexius shouted, his worry turning to anger.

"Nowhere!" Dean shouted back.

"I am your elder don't lie to me! Now where have you been?" Alexius stared him down.

"I was just walking and forgot the time, that's all," he wasn't really lying just not telling the whole truth.

Alexis sniffed the air a few times.

"But not alone Dean, who have you been with, I know it was a human. You know the danger they pose," he calmed slightly.

"Peter is not a danger to us, he's really nice," his voice sincere.

Alexius merely huffed in frustration; he knew Dean wasn't going to listen to him. He walked into the lodge, shaking his head. Dean followed, though he could understand what Alexius meant he couldn't just carry on his life with nobody by his side. Death would be preferable to the loneliness he would feel; he wouldn't live his life like that. But now wasn't the time to think about such things, the moon would soon be rising and it will be time for him to change. He couldn't have such thoughts. He went to his room to prepare, as he walked past Alexius' room he came to the door.

"Dean I'm sorry for going off on a rant, I understand you need a companion but you must be careful. I've been around for much longer than most, I know how such things can end," his eyes were staring at the floor. He was really sorry Dean could tell.

"It's alright Alex, I know you are only looking out for me," Dean smiled.

Alexius looked up and smiled warmly. Slapping Dean around the head lightly, "that's what mentors are supposed to do silly."

He could always lighten the mood; he was an expert at it. Dean just laughed softly shaking his head at his mentor's immaturity. Dean knew he was very old even by werewolf standards; however he had never gotten to his true age. Some of the things he accidentally lets slip draws Deans rough conclusion to ancient times.

He looked in his mid-forties but his body was unbelievably fit. He could even run rings round Dean. But he sometimes acted to young, at times bordering on that of a child. It pleased Dean to know that even when old a werewolf was still care free. He turned to go to his bedroom to get ready when Alexius slapped his arse with the back of his hand and laughed.

"Dammit Al you are sometimes such a child," he shouted out as he clenched at his buttocks.

"Don't be such a bloody baby," his laughter growing louder.

Dean turned to face him trying to turn his eyes all innocent, letting his bottom lip shake, and feigning sadness. This just made Alexius laugh harder, tears rolling down his cheeks. Dean laughed too.

"Go and get ready you, before you kill me from laughter," Alexius breathed out in between his cries of laughter.

Dean proceeded to his bedroom to prepare his body and mind for the change. It was still an ordeal for him; after all it was only three years since he was bitten. He laid down on his bed and tried to calm his mind, clear it off all thoughts. But time and time again his mind drifted back to Peter, and how much he had enjoyed walking and talking with him. He was happy to have a boyfriend. Could he tell him the truth he wondered, in time would he come to accept Dean for who he was and not for who he thought he was. It was hard lying to everyone, but he couldn't very well greet everyone with "Hi I'm Dean and I'm a werewolf, yeah you know the monsters in the old movies. Yeah well were real and I'm your neighbour." He didn't know how that would go, but he was sure it wouldn't be good. Shaking the thoughts from his mind in an attempt to relax and clear his head. He imagined himself in the dark forest, walking amongst the trees. Their lost leaves carpeting the ground, the smells surrounding him like a comforting blanket. He felt his heart beat slowly as ripple after ripple of stillness washed over him. He was running on all fours now, not chasing anything just running for the sheer joy of running. Soon his mind thought of nothing but the forest and its endless splendour of exciting possibilities. He heard a soft rapping on his door; he was broken out of his dream. Unbeknown to Dean he had fallen to sleep.

There was no sun coming from outside, darkness now covered the land. Pierced only by his night vision, he saw the town beyond the forest, its lights twinkling and glaring. His thoughts drifted back to Peter for a fleeting second before Dean pushed the thought to the back of his mind.

He rose from his bed, his joints ached all over. The first sign of the change, it wouldn't be long till he was a wolf and could play in the forest. But first he still had to go through the change, he hated the pain. He could feel the moons call, like the tide, for a werewolf it was irresistible. You just had to go to it, be covered by its light like a warm embrace. He felt a shiver of joy rush through his body. He opened the door to find Alexius naked with his back to him.

"You ready?" he asked without turning.

"Give me a few minutes I'm still dressed," as he rush back into his bedroom to undress.

"Last minute as usual," Alexius walked to the door to wait for Dean.

He came running from his bedroom likewise naked. It was easier this way they didn't have to worry about losing their clothes. They both stepped out into the welcoming darkness of the deep night, the only light coming from the almost perfect white orb that calmed their wolf spirits. The forest was bathed in a grey splendour, beckoning all off his kind to play and frolic. Dean felt the pain start, his wolf spirit eager to be released. Alexius saw the expression on Deans face change, he knew what was coming. He left Dean, giving him some privacy. It wasn't a nice experience at the best of times without someone watching. Dean started to turn before Alexis had left and screamed out in unbearable pain. His cries were horrible, he hadn't gotten used to the pain yet. His body was rearranging itself into the form of a large wolf. His bones moving and reshaping, the organs moving around in his body. The pain was a small trade-off for the freedom werewolves felt.

Chapter 11

He looked at the moon with his stark blue wolf eyes, his heart beat in his chest like the slow chug of a steam train, slow and powerful. He stretched out his muscles. Letting loose a little quiet howl, testing his vocal abilities and letting Alexis know he was alright. He looked out over the forest towards the city, its lights garish and polluting the fine beautiful darkness. However this night he was strangely drawn to it, to wander its streets. He wanted to look for something but he couldn't think what. There was something down there he needed to hunt, something he needed to stalk. But as to what could be urging him down there he didn't know. He felt his loins stir, PETER he had thought of Peter before he had changed. It still lingered in the back of his wolfs mind. It had interpreted it as Dean wishing to mate. The feeling growing unbearable and undeniable as his loins stirred further, the pinkish tip of his penis revealing itself from his fur sheath. No matter how hard he fought he knew it was pointless, the wolf's spirit would not be denied it's mating. He bounded off towards the city, his mind fixed on his quarry. Whether Peter liked it or not he would get a late night visitor.

He stopped at the edge of the road, he couldn't believe he was doing this it was insane. A huge wolf stalking the streets of a small but heavily populated town wasn't going to end well. He was across the road before he knew he had stepped out. His primal side taking over, he needed to remain in some sort of control, this was dangerous. He kept to the shadows and back streets, trying to avoid people where ever possible. Keeping close to the walls for safety, but if he was discovered it would be difficult to get out of here fast. Getting lost in these warren like alleys was easily done on the run. He put his nose to the ground trying to find any sign of him, any sort of scent he could pick up. But all he could smell in this alley was garbage and musty urine from both animals and human alike. He stalked through the dark streets, keeping his body close to the floor. All the while sniffing and testing the air for any sign of his prey. His mouth salivating as he caught a slight hint of Peter's scent. His mind went wild with the scent, his loins throbbing and trembling. He raced through the streets driven by animalistic lust, no longer caring whether he was seen or not. His rational side was screaming for him to stop and turn back to the safety of the dark forest. But instead his body kept on running. The stronger the scent got the more he got excited. He ran from the alley and onto a main street. It was full of people, he skidded to a halt and ducked back into the darkness before anybody saw him clearly. The ones that did catch a glimpse would think him nothing but a stray dog startled by the amount of people.

He backed off down the alley, his eyes fixed on the entrance just in case someone should investigate, bumping into a trash can, his bulk causing it to fall over with a clatter and spewing garbage across the alley's floor. There were voices and muffled shouting as a door was swung open. He heard footsteps coming closer. Finding himself trapped he assessed his options, if he ran up the alley he risked crashing into whoever was coming. If he doubled back he would run straight into the main street where there were dozens of people. Neither gave a very good chance of escape. He decided to try and hide in the dark shadows; his dull blonde coat would camouflage him well enough he hoped. A gate opened quietly and a group of three guys came out into the alley. Dean hadn't expected there to be more than one, and they looked a little menacing. He tried to press his body closer to the wall, the masonry cold on his skin. Stilling his breath he tried not to attract any more attention. The men spread out into the alley; one was brandishing a baseballs bat. He had a feeling this man was looking for trouble, he hoped they wouldn't see him. They scanned the dark alley looking for what had caused the noise. Dean smelt the stale stench of recently drunk beer on all of them. They were drunk out of their minds.

"Here kitty, kitty, kitty," one guy said in the dark alley.

"We won't hurts you honesth," the other slurring his words badly.

The man with the baseball bat remained silent; he seemed to be looking directly at Dean. He was looking at him; he motioned for his other friends and pointed directly at Dean. His heart started when he remembered a wolf's eyes reflect light and when he saw the lamp further up the alley he understood. They could see two circles of reflecting light, he had been spotted. But they thought it was a cat, so he was safe so far. But he couldn't leave without going through them.

"Come on kitty......we won't hurt you........." the man said trying to coax Dean out.

The man with the baseball bat moved towards Dean, he held back the urge to growl. He had to play his existence down; as far as they were concerned he was a cat so he had to keep that rouse going. As he drew closer he drew back the bat ready to hit Dean, he let loose a loud and menacing growl. A warning for the man to back off, it was filled with such venom and sounded so fierce echoing off the walls it even startled himself. The man with the bat jumped back two steps, his two friends doing the same. But it was just the shock of finding out it was a dog not a cat that made them jump. They were too pissed to realise dogs are more dangerous than cats. The man with the bat lunged at Dean going to strike at him. Dean jumped back out of the way of the bat, as he heard wood splinter on concrete he shot forward digging his canines in the man's throat. He dragged him like a rag doll into the light; he was still alive gurgling blood as he tried to defend himself. Dean clamped down with his jaws, crushing the man's throat with the ease of a cardboard tube. He didn't realise what he had done till it was too late and the man lay at his paws dead. His two other friends stared in horror at this huge wolf in the middle of town that had just killed their friend. They ran through the gate slamming it shut behind them. Dean wasn't interested in hurting anyone; he just wanted to see Peter. He ran off towards the forest as fast as he could no longer caring who saw him he had to get out of this town before he was caught. How could he tell Alexius, how would he understand. Simple he wouldn't, he had to wash before Alexis caught him covered in human blood. As he sped across the road by the forest leaving the town behind him he felt a little easier. But he couldn't believe what he had just done, he had just killed someone. He knew it was because he was threatening him and his wolf side had taken over to protect him. But if he wasn't there in the first place that person would still have been alive. He was dead because Dean had done something that Alexius warned him not to do; he had gotten close to a human. He was such a fool.

He laid in the river, washing the blood off his muzzle hoping Alexius couldn't smell it. Splashing about in the water in an attempt to wash the blood thoroughly from his fur, he heard a howl off in the distance; it was Alexius looking for him. Dean whimpered and continued washing. Another howl, closer this time. In order to buy himself more time he ran down the river, trying to get away from Alexis. He rolled about in the water, washing the rest of the evidence from his body. Now he had to hide the scent. He had to kill something to cover it up, setting off into the forest to search for an animal to hunt.

He had a deer in at his paws, chewing away angrily. Crushing bone and eating the organs, doing anything to hide the scent of human blood. Hearing rustling he looked up to see the silver fur of Alexius emerging from the undergrowth. When he didn't look angry or displeased, Dean hoped this meant he had succeeded in covering up the smell. Alexius came close and rubbed his snout against Dean's side, his way of saying hello. When there was no growl or other reprimand Dean calmed down glad he couldn't smell the blood previously covering his body. Alexius began to dig into the corpse as well, when Dean hunted he always left the heart for Alexius. He gobbled it up gratefully, blood matting his snout and dripping to the floor. All of a sudden Alexius stopped eating and his ears twitched. He could hear something in the distance. It sounded like police sirens, which in this town was quite rare. Shrugging it off he continued eating his meal. He had wondered where Dean had got to but the kill at his paws answered that question. He had howled to him but he hadn't answered. But then he was in a strange mood tonight, he thought maybe the argument earlier had upset him more than he was letting on. When they had finished eating they both went for a walk, too full to run comfortably.

The moon was still high in the sky when they first heard the trucks arriving and passing by. Which was strange there shouldn't be any traffic on the small roads at this time of night. They both decided to stay off the roads till the morning. They didn't want to attract unwanted attention. Dean saw lights flashing inside the woods, like torches. His eyes grew wide in fear and shock. He whimpered to Alexius who turned and saw them too, his eyes growing wide. There shouldn't be people in this forest it was protected by law and the people in town respected the law. In all the years he lived here nobody had entered this forest at night. He could hear people walking through the undergrowth, and a loud click. He knew what that was; it was the cocking of a rifle. Alexius turned to Dean quickly and barked at him to run as the first shot rang out. Dean didn't argue and ran as fast as his legs could carry him, not waiting for Alexius. He was trying to keep his head down as not to catch a bullet in the back on the head. Another shot rang out, flying close to him. They were in relative open, not many trees in this part of the forest more shrubbery than anything else. Even though he was worried about Alexius he had to keep running. A moment's hesitation could be his last moment on earth. He could hear men shouting and swearing. Another shot, this one was closer to him this time. He could hear their voices but he couldn't understand them from this distance. Every part of his mind and body was concerned only with survival. The hunters were behind him, but they couldn't keep up with a werewolf. He was starting to build up a sizable lead on the humans. Catching a glimpse of silver out of one eye he stole a quick glance to his right. He could see the bushes move and a silver shape dart past the gaps. Glad his mentor had gotten away the worry he felt since the first shot began to subside. The worry he had felt since the hunt began now subsided.

There was another shot Dean heard it whistle past his ear followed by a loud yip. He saw Alexius' form slump to the ground but he didn't get up. Dean skidded to a halt, slipping on the soft, damp ground. He ran over to his mentor, worried for his safety. Running through the bushes, the gunshots stopped. They must think they had got their target. Dean prodded Alexius with his snout, but there was no movement. He listened for any breathing a heartbeat anything that could tell him whether he lived or died. But there was nothing, he was dead, killed by a stray bullet. Dean shouted at the top of his lungs a cry of utter horror and anger. It came out as a heart chilling howl that reverberated in his chest, hurting his vocal cords. He turned to face the hunters that now advanced on his friend's stricken body. Seeing nothing but red his every breath becoming an angry growl of purest hatred, he shot towards his mentors murderers, bent on their deaths. Springing from a bush he caught the first by the arm, his jaws clamping down crushing bone. He pulled him off his feet and ripped chunks from his flesh. Before he could finish the first man off another walked from the bushes. Dean could see from his uniform it was a local police officer. He was only young; maybe twenty but Dean didn't care. He was dead all the same; he attacked before he could unbutton his holster. Grabbing the young officer by his hip he tugged and tore at the flesh. The man took out a knife and stuck it in Dean's shoulder, the blade slicing through the edge of his shoulder blade. He shrugged the pain off, his anger blocking all other sensations but their death screams. He tore out chunks of his chest, crunching up his rib bones and ripping his lungs from the cavity while the young man still lived. Looking at the young man in his cold dead eyes shook Dean back to his senses. What was he doing, he had killed these men, killed them in cold blood. He ran away from their bodies into the dark night, even the moon hiding from Dean's carnage. Dean grabbed Alexius' body by the scruff off his neck and dragged him away from the hunters. His body would remain in wolf form till the moon set and the sun rose at which point it would revert back to its human form. He couldn't make it to the lodge till morning, but they had a small hideout in a cave should they need to hide. Dean dragged the body there, his shoulder grating with every movement as the knife that was still stuck in him sliced more into his shoulder blade. When he finally got his masters body back to safety he took the knife in his jaws and pulled it out, blood ran down his leg dripping to the floor. He howled in agony that had been kept at bay by the adrenaline that pumped through his veins.

He slumped down on Alexius' body and whimpered in sadness, he cried silently but no tears came from his eyes. But if he could he would have cried himself to sleep, the pain and exhaustion overwhelming him, forcing him to drop into a state of unconsciousness.

He awoke the next morning still sprawled on top of the body of his mentor. He could see now what killed him; he had taken a bullet to the heart. Now he cried as he took Alexius' body in his arms and carried him to their lodge, taking care not to be seen. When he got there he knew it would be found, and if they should do a post mortem on the body they would find out all about his kind. Alexius wouldn't become some local coroners Nobel Prize nomination. Laying his body carefully on the bed Dean placed his hand on Alexius' head. He dropped to his knees in fits of hysteria, his sobs and wails utterly horrible to hear. Through the tears he tried to say he was sorry, but the words just wouldn't form. He had to leave as soon as possible before the hunters from last night found this place. After stuffing as much of his things he could in a rucksack he stood in the room forming a plan. Quickly lighting a fire in the fireplace he threw as much firewood in the grate as it would hold and kicked the rest as close as he could. He said his goodbyes to Alexius and let the fire consume the lodge. He didn't look back till he was half way past town, the cloud of smoke was drifting high. The fire must have been raging by now destroying all evidence.

He dropped his head low and carried on walking. He would leave his old life behind and lead his own. Never again will he let things get out of hand. It was his fault Alexius was dead, he had heard in town of the hunters being sent out after a rabid wolf that had killed a man in town. He was the cause of all this, all because he didn't listen to his teacher, because he didn't follow the rules. Well from now on he would, to the letter.

Chapter 12

Dean looked over to Edmund after completing his story, his eyes brimming with tears as he remembered the horror he had caused. He had tried his best to forget the past these four years. However Edmund deserved to know the truth, he needed to know about Dean's dark past. Secrets were never good in any relationship. He eyed Edmund carefully looking for any sign of what he was thinking. He was clearly shocked by the revelation but still seemed to be digesting what he had heard. His eyes narrow in thought.

"Dean what did you do, you could have revealed our secret;" he stood and looked down at his younger lover waiting for an explanation.

But Dean had none; he had been stupid that night. And he had gotten his mentor killed, all over a human he liked. Because he wanted a boyfriend and some sort of resemblance to a normal life. It was a selfish want when compared to the needs and safety of an entire species. But at the time he hadn't thought about that, he didn't think about much spare his own desires. And for those desires he had gotten the only person he had in his life killed. He was ashamed at what he had done. Dean had never forgiven himself so he had no right to expect Edmund to forgive him. But he hoped he could, he didn't know what he would do if he couldn't.

"Edmund forgive me please, I never wanted anyone hurt. I was an idiot and should never have gone to town that night," he pleaded.

"You put us all in danger, including me," Edmund lowered his eyes to the floor, he was hurt.

Dean sobbed loudly, "Please forgive me!" whilst clinging onto Edmunds hand tightly.

"Dean I need to think about this," Deans sobbing cutting at his heart.

Edmund pulled away from Dean and headed to the door. Dean was still crying for him to forgive him and sobbing when he closed the door behind him. He trudged down the stairs in a near

103

daze, thinking about what he had just been told. He left Deans building and looked up at the setting sun. Its rays dying as the night started to advance. He needed to think about this, so he headed towards the forest the only place he honestly felt at peace. The trees canopy rustled in the slight breeze, the floor carpeted by now browning leaves as fall rapidly approached. Their forms crunching under Edmunds feet, and swirled as the breeze whipped them up in an intricate dance to an invisible and uncaring audience. Even Edmund was untouched by the dusk's beauty at the moment, its facets of splendour going unnoticed.

He had to think about what he had been told he felt like he did truly love Dean. But finding out someone you thought you loved had murdered two men in blind rage was a lot to take in. His mind was awash with emotion, anger, pity, love, worry. He couldn't think straight. The man in the alley was just self-defence, the wolf side of Dean would have done that without him even thinking about it, acting on a basic and pure survival instinct. But the two men later that night was fuelled by nothing but vengeance and anger. Could he be forgiven for that? Could Edmund forgive him for that, he was unsure if he honestly could. What had drawn Dean to do something so out of character. Was it just vengeance or was it something else that drove him to commit such a horrific act. What did Dean feel for Alexius, he knew he looked up to him like a father but could he have loved him as a father. If he did then that would explain why he reacted so foolishly. He remembered how Dean had spoken of Alexius, the look in his eyes. Yes sorrow and guilt, but also there was a love there. It did seem to Edmund that Dean loved this Alexius as a father, after all he had shown Dean as much paternal protection and worry as Dean had shown him a son's love. Edmund thought more on this. Taking a seat on a felled log he followed this train of thought. Yes Dean could be excused for reacting like that not just in anger but also grief at losing his substitute father. He could understand it, if that had happened to Edmund at such a young age, not only in human years but in werewolf years, would he have done things differently. He didn't know, he hoped he would be strong enough not to take a human life, but he wasn't sure if he could. Could anybody be sure of how they would react at losing the closest thing to a parent you had known since you had a great upheaval that had changed your entire life. Nobody could possibly know how they would react under such conditions at Dean's age and with his horrific past. It was a wonder the young man was still sane.

He walked through the forest thinking about how Dean must have felt when his mentor died, when he realised he had killed those men. The fear and horror he must have been feeling. He was no longer angry, he felt sorry for Dean. It must have been the shock upon hearing it. He looked up at the sky; night was soon starting to fall. He could already see the moons ghostly visage showing through the dark red sky. Starting his walk back into town the sun had dipped past the horizon leaving just the dull afterglow behind, the glorious night starting to overpower the bright daylight.

Edmund stood at the door to Dean's apartment. How could he have walked out on him when he needed comfort the most? It was so insensitive of him. Twice he ran away from him scared. He was petrified of getting too close to someone again. He had been alone for such a long time, drifting from one area to another, never stopping to get to know anybody, till he met Dean. And for some reason he couldn't leave him now. He seemed to be almost drawn to him, tied to him, and bound to him. Anybody else he wouldn't have let himself get this close, but it had happened so quick yet so subtly he hadn't noticed. He knocked on the door lightly. But he knew to Dean's ears it would be like he was pounding on the door. He could hear Dean walking to door, as he opened it Edmund could see he had been crying a lot. His eyes were red and rubbed raw, his cheeks damp with spent tears. When he looked at Edmund it was with deep sadness and regret. Who had to wonder whether he was regretting what he had done or telling him, or maybe both. Dean started to sob slightly when he saw Edmund, he held out his arms to him. He wanted to be held, he needed some comfort. Edmund put his arms around Dean, lifting him from the floor as he swept him into the apartment closing the door with his foot. Dean's sobs became a flood off tears as all his emotions were released. Edmund sat on the sofa with Dean in his lap, his arms wrapped around his crying lover. Just from the tender way he was being held Dean knew he had been forgiven. Edmund had forgiven him, but he was unsure whether he could forgive himself. For all these years he hadn't been able to, maybe now someone else had forgave him, he could.

"I didn't think you would come back," Dean's voice trembled as he cried.

Edmund choked back his own tears, "I understand how you must have felt."

"Do you forgive me?" his eyes almost pleading.

Edmund kissed Dean lightly on the forehead, "yes I do."

Dean threw his arms round Edmund and hugged him tightly. As he laid his head on Edmunds strong muscular shoulder Dean felt much better, the weight of his past lifting from his shoulders. His eyes closed as he felt every muscle, his entire body relax in Edmunds warm embrace.

"Edmund I need closure on this. I need to accept what I did and also accept the consequences. I need to turn myself in," his eyes searching Edmunds for some sort of answer.

Edmund just nodded, he knew what Dean was saying. He wanted to face up to what he did, that was the only way he could put it behind him. Admitting it to himself was the first step, now he had to answer for what he did. He had to stand before them and face their judgement and whatever punishment they deemed necessary.

"So I want to see the werewolf council," he simply stated.

Edmund nodded his head; though he didn't want Dean to face their punishment, it was the only way he could be rid of what he did. He just hoped they would be easy on him; he didn't like the council all that much. They were easily corrupted by the power they could wield and this was a very serious crime.

"Not yet, it's getting late and I think we both need some sleep, come on lets go back to bed," Edmund took Dean by his hand and guided him back into the bedroom.

The suns light shone in the room, its bright reddish tones colouring Edmunds bare muscular torso in a dull orange. Dean watched as his strong chest rose and fell slowly as he breathed lightly. He looked very peaceful all night, like he wanted to be next to Dean. He had even got snuggled up close to him during the night.

Dean had missed the affection and intimacy of sleeping with another man; it was like no other feeling. Safe and warm yet just that little bit scary. It seemed Dean being honest with Edmund had brought them closer together. Dean laid his arm over Edmunds stomach and laid his head on his strong chest. He soon drifted off to sleep. His dreams were of a beautiful woman who stood above him, framed by the full moon. She felt his pain, his worry. Laying a cool, soft hand on his forehead the worry soon lifted. When she spoke he heard no words but understood her all the same. She simply said "Be still my sweet child, the moon shall watch over you. Even during the day her presence will be revealed to you. Look to her when you find yourself surrounded by darkness and bask in her light." Then she was gone, replaced by a beautiful moonlit forest, his forest, his home, his kingdom.

Chapter 13

He was awoken by someone shaking his shoulder gently; he could hear someone calling out his name softly. He opened his eyes slowly, sleep making his vision blurred. Though he couldn't see who was above him he knew who it was from their gentle touch. Edmund was trying to rouse him, as he drove away the grogginess in his mind he noticed it was still daylight. He looked at the digital clock that was beside his bed, its stark light said it was 11:02. As he pulled himself up off the bed Edmund swept his hand away causing him to fall over and roll to the floor. Edmund laughed and ran out of the room. Even though his hip hurt Dean couldn't help but laugh. One hundred and forty six years old and he still acted like a child at times; Dean shook his head as he picked himself up off the floor. He had grazed his hip on the corner off the bed, but to a werewolf such a wound was nothing it would be healed in a matter of hours, striding out into the living space, without a stitch on his body. He put his hands on his hips and glared at Edmund, trying to look as serious as he could, his eyes hard and not a hint of a smile. Edmund just stared at him, his eyes wide, then all off a sudden he just burst out laughing, nearly dropping his coffee in the process.

"This isn't funny, it's serious, you hurt me," Dean pointed at the graze that started at his hip and curled over his rump.

"I'm sorry," he said through his laughter, "but I just couldn't help it."

"You're like a big kid; I can't believe you're over one hundred years old. Act more like your age," Dean chuckled and shook his head.

"Ok then I will," Edmund grabbed his heart and fell to the floor holding his breath, feigning death.

Dean walked over and kicked him in the side hard. Payback for the graze he had caused. Edmund grabbed Dean's ankle and pulled him off balance, he fell on top of his lover knocking the wind out of him. Dean wrestled his leg out of Edmunds grip, straddled his waist and gave him a smug look.

"Well that didn't quite go as I planned," he gasped out as he caught his breath.

Edmund laid his hands on Dean's bare hips, stroking the mark he had left with one finger. He looked into the other man's eyes thoughtfully and smiled. Dean leant forward and kissed him lightly on the lips. They kissed for what seemed a life time. Their lips locked in tender, sweet love.

"I think I had better get dressed," Dean whispered in Edmunds ear after pulling himself from the kiss.

As he stood he helped Edmund up off the floor. He walked into the bedroom, his legs trembling slightly. He was afraid of what would happen today, would he be forgiven as easily as he had been by Edmund. He wasn't sure; it was the not knowing that was killing him. Trying to guess which way they would decide. If they didn't forgive him, how would they punish him? It was more than just fear; he was petrified of what was to come. But he also knew that while ever he was with Edmund he would be fine, no matter the punishment the council cast on him. Quickly getting dressed, he wanted to make a good impression so he chose smart clothes. But nothing overly smart, a white shirt over a black t-shirt, the top button undone with a loosely tied tie round his neck. His best pair of designer jeans and some new brown shoes he had picked up after work one afternoon. He walked out of the bedroom, ready for what they might throw at him. He heard a wolf whistle from the window. Turning to see Edmund leant on the sill admiring him.

"Ok now you look seriously sexy," his grin grew wider but it was a genuine smile.

"Why thank you," Dean pulled a sexy pose, blowing Edmund a kiss.

Edmund chuckled and shook his head. He felt alive with Dean, more alive than he had felt for a long time. He brought a sparkle to the world; he brought a sparkle to his world. His every word, his every action brought with it a wonder he had rarely seen. So naive yet he had experienced and felt things most werewolves hadn't in their century long lives. He had fallen for him, fallen deeply and madly in love with him. And after only a couple of days, he had never experienced this feeling before. Sure he had loved people in his life, but never this strongly, never so utterly and completely. He wanted to spend all his immortal life with this person. And now he was delivering him into a strange and unfamiliar community, where he would be judged by people who do not even know him. Though he didn't want to do it, he had to. Dean had been right last night he had to face what he did, otherwise it would forever hang over his head. Edmund just hoped they would understand. After all he was only young, scared and his substitute father had just been killed. He reacted wrongly, but it was understandable.

"Right you Mr, whose car, are we taking, yours or mine?" Edmund asked grinning.

"Erm we can take mine if you want, it's the closest," he smiled weakly, but Edmund could see he was worried.

Edmund put his arm round Dean's shoulder, pulling him close while they walked to the door. As they opened it they saw Deans next door neighbour Val open hers. She looked at Dean and then at Edmund her eyes slightly wide at the fact she had finally seen someone else at his. But the way they were holding each other. He took her a few seconds to fully understand, but when she did her eyes grew wider. She opened her mouth to say something but she was in such shock nothing would come out. For the first time Dean had known her she couldn't find anything to say. Dean and Edmund gave her a slight smile and walked off down the stairs their smiles growing wider. Dean laid his head upon Edmunds shoulder. The door to his apartment clicking shut, the catch popping and all the while Val still stood stock still in disbelief.

Chapter 14

A jolt knocked Dean awake, his head banging on the car window. He must have fallen asleep. He looked over to see Edmund driving, he seemed exhausted too. His buttocks had gone numb causing him to fidget uncomfortably. He placed a hand on Edmunds thigh lightly, letting him know he was awake. His lover turned to look at him and smiled warmly. Dean smiled back; his eyes though looking weary, twinkled. Edmund put his arm round Dean's shoulder and pulled him closer, kissing him on the forehead. Dean smiled as he snuggled in to Edmunds shoulder. Dean looked out of the driver's side window; they were passing through a vast forest comprised of majestic and regal redwoods dotted with a few ash trees. It was beautiful and untouched; Dean longed to walk through its shadowy paths with Edmund. To sit with him by its lakes and rivers, climb its hills. As he watched the forest pass by through the window, an unsettling feeling of familiarity washed over him. Even though he has never been here before, he felt like he knew it, knew every tree and every boulder. But he couldn't work out why. He shook the thoughts out of his head. He had bigger things to worry about.

Dean cuddled deeper into Edmunds shoulder; it was a column shift car so there was nothing to keep them apart. He pulled Dean closer towards him, his grip growing stronger, more protective. It was due to this Dean realised they must have been getting close to the enclave. He was right; he soon started to see signs for a town called Howling Falls, probably a werewolf's idea of a joke. As they got closer the forest became thicker, older and more natural. It was obviously not kept for humans but for werewolves, providing more off a natural habitat for them. To a human it would be dark and foreboding yet to a werewolf it was incredibly inviting.

Edmund slowed down as the road narrowed. Signs dotted the road warning that the forest was private property and trespassers would be prosecuted. The road grew more unkempt, becoming darker as overhanging tree branches blocked out the bright sunlight. Then as they got further down the lane he was blinded by beautiful sunshine. There was a huge clearing, devoid of trees. The bright blue sky dotted with a few wispy white clouds. It was amazing after the darkened drive they had taken through the forest. To his left were places for cars to be parked, there were a few cars in places but there were many more unoccupied spaces. Edmund pulled into one of these. As he put the car into park and turned off the engine he turned towards Dean. He looked at him, his eyes soft and emotional.

"You know I'm always here for you, no matter how they punish you. Ok," his voice quiet.

Dean didn't say anything he just threw his arms round Edmunds chest tightly. Hugging him like it was the last hug he would receive. Edmund stroked at his hair to let him know there was nothing to worry about.

"I know you won't leave me Edmund, that's the only reason I'm willing to do this," his cheek on the strong shoulder of his partner.

Dean lifted his head from Edmund shoulder, his eyes glistening with small tears. But he soon shook them from his eyes, wiped his cheeks and nodded to Edmund that he was ready. Dean opened the door and stepped out on the gravel parking area. A cool breeze of late afternoon air swirled around them, with it came a dusting of familiar and new smells. The sharp tang of tree pollen, the faint perfume of sweet smelling flowers and the over powering stench of werewolves. The smells burned into his mind and relaxed each muscle. He was among friends here, not enemies. He didn't have to worry about being himself. Edmund saw his shoulders physically drop as the tension was soon washed away. He inhaled the scents that surrounded him; he belonged here with others of his kind, with his fellow werewolves.

Edmund put his arm around his slender shoulders pulling him closer, ready to guide Dean to meet the council. They walked towards the large cast iron gate, it was intimidating. A great stone wall surrounded the entire town except at either side leading to the forest. Easy access for when the moon entered its fullest cycle. They both walked up the drive slowly towards the huge black gate, at one side stood a guard, dressed in a blue security uniform. Dean could smell he was a werewolf, an old one too, but not as old as Edmund. As they got to the gate he stopped them, putting his arm out. He gave them a sniff and nodded.

"How can I help you today brothers?" he asked.

"We have an audience with the council. I telephoned and explained the situation on our drive up," Edmund responded.

"Oh yes. I was informed to expect you. I'm afraid the council chambers are closed now, but they will see you tomorrow," he sounded apologetic.

Dean and Edmund nodded to him as they were allowed through the gates. The cobbled surface rough, old and uneven beneath their feet, everything about this place smelt of old to Dean. Everything even the buildings themselves were permeated with the smell, the smell of old werewolves. Some dead and gone; others still here. Dean wondered what they would be like, would they be fun or serious. He had only known 2 other werewolves up to now. Maybe it was time he had some friends of his own kind instead of human acquaintances. Casting his gaze around at the buildings, all being made off old greying wood. Old colonial in style but he could tell they weren't reproductions. They were original, built somewhere between the 1700's and the 1800's if he had to guess. Another thing that struck him was the lack of people. It was empty. Nobody walking the paths, it seemed deserted.

They heard voices coming from one of the side paths that lead to the main street they were on. There was an angry male voice followed by the squeal and giggling of a young girl. Both Dean and Edmund turned in curiosity, a young looking woman came running out of the path almost bowling Dean over. She had a large smile, though turning red after bumping into Dean. Her bright green eyes flashed with amusement, her long red hair cascading down past her waist, glinting in the strong sunlight. They heard the thudding of feet coming down the path, the girl hid and took refuge behind Dean. A few seconds later an equally young looking man ran from the direction she had come. He was about to open his mouth to speak when he caught a glimpse of the young woman hid behind Dean. Pointing an accusing finger he advanced.

"Clarice, you are so going to get it," He shouted.

Clarice ducked back behind Dean for protection like a child. Dean put up a hand to the man who stopped and looked perplexed.

"I'm not going to let you hurt her," Dean said forcefully.

To Dean's surprise the man burst out laughing followed by the girl behind him. It was then he noticed the man bore the same flame red hair as the girl and vivid green eyes. He was covered in mud and had leaves stuck in his dishevelled hair.

"She's my twin sister; she pushed me into the garden that's why I was mad. I wouldn't really have hurt her, besides I'm not really that mad," he said still chuckling as his sister came from behind Dean and stood next to her brother holding his arm.

He picked the leaves out of his hair and rubbed at the muck on his jeans. His hands were covered in the sticky brown mess, playfully smudging his sister's nose with it, she didn't realise what he had done and just pushed him. She smiled at Dean who smiled back trying not to laugh at the mark on her face. Edmund looked away and Dean heard him laughing under his breath.

"Is there something on my face," she asked innocently.

This was too much and all three men burst out laughing as her brother tried to tell her what he had done. But in his laughter all he could do was point at her face. Turning she looked at her reflection in the window and started at the realisation. She stared at her brother through narrowed eyes.

"Andre'! I hate you!" she shouted as she glared at him.

He tried to stop laughing and be more serious about it but he couldn't. It just made him laugh harder. She kicked him hard in the shin; he hopped up and down in pain but still continued to laugh. She was about to storm off when Dean put up his hands and stopped her. He licked his thumb dampening the skin, cleaning the mud off her nose in one movement rubbing it on his jeans. He smiled at her warmly. She smiled back.

"Thanks, what's your name?" Clarice asked.

"Erm Dean, and this is Edmund," he said nodding in his partner's direction.

116

She nodded at Edmund who smiled back as warmly as Dean had earlier. She saw him glance at Dean, his eyes alone conveying more love than she had ever witnessed, a palpable wave of emotion. Her eyebrows raised and her smile grew wider as the realisation they were lovers came over her. But they were more than just lovers; they seemed to be soul mates. She could almost feel the love that they both felt for one another. She was happy for them both but also slightly envious of the love that they had. She longed to be loved in that way, so completely. Edmund noticed the way her demeanour had changed, he looked at her puzzled. Something in her eyes twinkled as she motioned at Dean with them. Edmund grinned from ear to ear as he realised she knew and nodded to confirm it. She grew slightly giddy as she nodded towards Dean and then at Edmund. Edmund again nodded to confirm that Dean loved him too. She gave out a little squeal of delight and clapped her hands together. Andre' and Dean fixed their eyes on her totally confused and waiting for an explanation.

"They're lovers Andre', they're together," she shouted excitedly.

"But how......................," Dean began to ask.

"It's obvious with your eyes, the way you look at each other with such heartfelt love," she said giddily.

"So not so much werewolves than a couple of queerwolves eh?" Andre' playfully asked.

Dean rolled his eyes while Edmund just smirked. His sister slapped hard on the back of his head and shook her head in disapproval. Dean also shook his head, but only at the fact the joke was terrible.

"That joke was utterly rubbish," he remarked still shaking his head.

"Yeah if that's the best you have I shouldn't tell any joke, for all eternity," Edmund jokingly added.

117

Clarice giggled at her brother's embarrassment as he put up his hands defensively. He smiled and nodded in way of an apology.

"Hey why don't you both meet us for drinks tonight at the Wolfen Arms," Andre' asked, "Then you can check in to the hotel next door."

"Thanks we will," Dean said feeling easier about his time here.

They all said their goodbyes till later that evening, then Dean and Edmund went to rent a room for a few nights at the hotel Andre' had told them about. They both trudged up the heavily carpeted stairs heading to their room, each wooden step creaking, betraying their age. What must have once been a dark and gloomy staircase was now lit by hanging chandeliers, the light reflecting from the glass of the multiple pictures that adorned the walls. Paintings of wolves frolicking in the moonlight, each painted in a different style popularised by that time period. Traditional, fine art, modernism, impressionism, abstract, expressionism, photorealism and surrealism, it was all there. Showing how long this hotel had been catering for their kind. They got to their room and Edmund slipped the old iron key into the lock, the clunking loud and heavy. As he swung the door open they were bathed in the deep red of the setting sun, its colour casting its hue on everything it touched. The room became a range of muted red tones. Edmund walked in, looking around at the small room. Its double bed looked soft and comfortable, its dark green bed clothes turning almost black in the light. Dean heaved his heavy bag next to the bed, he felt weary from the long drive. He looked over at Edmund who looked beyond tired, his eyelids heavy with exhaustion. He sighed and dropped onto the bed, falling onto his back. He closed his eyes and let out a loud sigh of relief at the comfort he felt. Dean kicked the door shut and climbed onto the bed with him, snuggling up close to his warm body. His arm draped over his chest, pulling him closer. He kissed Edmund lightly on the lips and laid his head on his strong shoulder. They were both very tired from the long drive and the worry they had both felt. It wasn't long till they were both snoring lightly in their warm embrace.

When Dean awoke, it was pitch black in the room. It was the middle of the night. He could still feel Edmund next him, his snoring telling him he was asleep still. But he couldn't see anything; he laid his head back on Edmund's shoulder and kissed his neck softly. This woke Edmund slightly; he moved his shoulder and pulled Dean closer to him. Half kissing him on the cheek before settling back down to sleep, Dean let his hand wander lower on Edmunds body, snaking it under his shirt. Feeling the rippling muscle that lay beneath the modest covering before running his finger round the navel. He heard Edmund let out a small sigh of contentment. Dean nuzzled into his neck a little and kissed the soft skin. Edmund moaned quietly, turning so that they were facing one another. He could feel the warm breath on his lips as Edmund moved in to kiss Dean. He kissed him with such passion it took his breath away. But mingled in that passion there was also love, Clarice was right, it was obvious how much they felt for one another.

"I love you," Dean's voice seemed so quiet as he said it, that if Edmund had not been a werewolf he wouldn't have heard it.

"Dean when I first saw you that night, it was the night love took a hold of my heart. You mean everything to me now, and I'm not going to lose you," he whispered it so softly, but it spoke louder than any shout to Deans ears.

He felt tears swell in his eyes; t was the first time Edmund had shown that amount of emotion towards anyone. But just Dean telling him he loved him was strong enough to break down the walls he had created. It smashed them down as though they were made of paper. He sniffed a couple of times, tears of joy and love. Dean realised he was crying, he wiped away the tears from Edmunds eyes kissing him softly on the forehead. Edmund moved closer, kissing Dean lightly on the neck. His scent rising in his nostrils, stirring his blood and his lust, he pushed Dean onto his back, slowly undoing his tie dropping it over the side of the bed. He unbuttoned his shirt, button by agonising button. Opening it out, Dean shuffled and slipped it off his arms throwing it to one side. Edmund straddled Dean's waist, lifting up his t-shirt and pulling it off over his head. His mid length brown-blonde hair falling down covering his eyes, he moved the obstruction away with his finger, revealing his luminescent blue eyes almost glowing in the dim light. Edmund slowly undid the buckle on Dean's belt, pulling it out of his jeans in one movement.

"You've done that before haven't you," Dean said laughing.

"I've had some practice with belts yes," Edmund replied stroking Dean's hair softly.

Dean laughed as Edmund lent close to kiss him on the lips, their eyes closed. Then Edmund moved lower down Dean's body with his lips, kissing at his chest. Moving further down kissing at his slim but muscled stomach, Dean moaned as he played with Edmunds long black hair, twirling its strands round his fingers. Edmund undid the button on Dean's jeans, all the while kissing at his stomach. His tongue probing and skirting the edge of his navel, Dean shuffled and lifted his buttocks as Edmund pulled his jeans down, whipping them off his ankles. Edmund quickly pulled his shirt off over his head without undoing the buttons. He was about to take off his jeans when Dean sat up and stopped him. He stroked at Edmunds heavily muscled torso, his hands roaming till they got to his waistband. Dean quickly found his button in the darkness, popping it open and slowly unzipped his fly. He let the jeans just drop to the floor, Edmund stepped out of them and advanced on Dean who laid back on the bed again. He once again straddled the younger man's waist, whose penis was already erect. Edmund could feel it against his tight muscular buttocks. He took a firm grip of its shaft and guided it to its target. He felt its tip on his rectum, he was thankful for the pre-ejaculate providing some lubrication. He lowered himself down on the hard rod, its stiff form invading the soft flesh of Edmunds rectum. He moaned loudly as the last of its length slipped inside him. Dean gasped from the pleasure that shot down from its head. Edmund placed his hands on Dean's chest, caressing his soft smooth skin as he lifted himself up. Then lowered himself back down slowly, moaning loudly, Dean groaning with pleasure. Edmund began to rock, fast and steady. His face screwed up with pleasure, he moaned louder and louder as his orgasm built. Dean's legs shuffled as he felt his own pleasure growing. He placed his hands on Edmunds hips and urged him to go faster. He obliged with grunts as he rocked faster and faster. Dean could feel his ejaculation nearing; it wouldn't be long till he was brought to orgasm. Then he shouted out in pleasure as his semen shot in the great spurts. Edmund felt the warm thick liquid coat his insides, he moaned and gasped as he slowed his pace. He lent forward to kiss Dean lovingly on the lips before pulling himself free from Dean. He dropped to the bed tired out; he snuggled up to Dean who was still on his back reeling from his orgasm. He draped an arm over Dean's chest and pulled him closer. They embraced till they both dropped to sleep, snoring heavily as their exhaustion took over them.

Chapter 15

The dawning sun shone through the window, filling the room with new orange light. A solitary figure stood dressed in only a pair of jeans, his bare torso warmed by the sun's rays. Dean turned when he heard Edmund turn over in bed, he was totally uncovered. They had knocked the covers off the bed the night before in their passion, both being too tired to pick them up afterwards. Scooping them up he threw them on top of him, tucking him in and kissing his cheek lightly as not to wake him. He hadn't gotten much sleep; his worry about today's meeting with the council waking him every other hour. Feeling sleep nagging at him from behind his eyes and the back off his neck, he just ignored it. There was no way he could sleep at the moment. When he had no idea what was going to happen to him. He was scared of the judgment that was hanging over his head. He didn't know what it would be, but he knew they wouldn't let him go without some sort of punishment.

He felt someone touch the bottom of his bare back, the warm fingers running down his exposed rump. He looked to see Edmund leant on his elbow in bed, the covers barely covering his bottom half. He smiled at Dean warmly motioning for him to come back to bed. Dean undid his jeans and dropped them. He slipped under the covers, the bed warm from Edmunds hunky body. He laid his head on Edmunds outstretched arm and huddled closer to his partner. Either for comfort or security he didn't know, maybe it was both. He was worried about being punished by the council but he was far more worried about losing Edmund. He had only just found him and he wasn't going to let him go without some sort of a fight. He huddled in closer and clung to the other man; he was not going to let him go.

Later that morning an insistent tapping at the door awoke Edmund from his shallow slumber. He blinked out the sleep that remained in his eyes, the bright morning sun making him squint. He stretched out his body the muscles aching a joint popping. Looking towards Dean to see he was still fast asleep, he was glad he needed it. Edmund had heard him tossing and turning next to him before getting up not long after dawn. He eased his arm from under Dean's head, slowly so he didn't wake him. He threw on his jeans and almost crept towards the door. The tapping had gotten harder and more impatient. Edmund unlocked the door, as soon as the person on the other side heard the mortise slide back and the key click they

123

stopped knocking. Edmund opened the door, to find a young looking man on the other side. His eyes were soft and gentle; he smiled a naive sort of grin towards Edmund. He was dressed in a dark grey suit, with a pure white shirt and a red tie. The man offered his hand to Edmund who shook it briskly. He bowed his head slightly and passed Edmund a cylinder. Its surface engraved with an intricate pattern, its ends adorned with ornate finials, a scroll case. The young runner bowed his head again and retreated from the door, trotting downstairs. Edmund closed the door and examined the scroll, it was beautiful. But it was a beauty that could hold a terrible fate for Dean. He began to unscrew the scroll from its casing when he looked over towards Dean. He should be awake when it was opened; after all it was his fate that it contained. Placing the scroll on the bedside table, its heavy metal form clunking loudly, the sound did little to stir Dean from his heavy sleep, having not slept for half the night. Edmund placed a hand firmly on Dean's shoulder and shook him gently, when he didn't respond he shook with more force. This time round he started to wake, so Edmund shook him again this time not as hard. Dean opened his eyes, blinking a few times. When he saw it was Edmund a drowsy half smile spread across his face as he stretched out his body.

"Good morning sexy," Dean yawned out.

"Good morning yourself," Edmund kissed Dean lightly on the lips.

Edmund sat down on the bed next to Dean; he took the scroll in his hand and offered it to Dean. Who looked perplexed by its strange form and appearance. The unusual patterns engraved on its cylindrical surface. The twisted leaves of the ornate rococo finials, each carved by hand. It was truly a magnificent piece of craftsmanship. However it petrified Dean more than anything ever had, for what it contained has been a source of horror for him for two days. He took it from Edmund gingerly, its form heavy and cold, possibly the same as their judgement. He began to unscrew the end, as he did so he noticed the other finial turning at the same time. They were connected, the finials were the scroll. It creaked as he continued to unscrew the scroll from its case. Clicking as the cap came away from its threads inside the case. Dean carefully pulled out the scroll as though it was the charge from a bomb, he dared not look at it but he knew he must. He slowly pulled the paper scroll down, its layers unravelling and revealing the text that lay beneath. It was written in a spidery but legible hand. It was cordially inviting Dean and Edmund to the council chambers this afternoon to discuss their unusual predicament. They were to be seen by the council at three pm sharp. Dean looked at the clock that lay beside the bed. It was now eleven thirty two am, in just under four hours he was to find out his fate. Though the wording of the invite gave Dean hope they would be lenient. He passed the scroll to Edmund after he had finished reading it, he himself casting his eyes over it. He scanned the words quickly before handing it back to Dean. Dean read through it once more. Surprised at the politeness of the words, it shocked him; he expected a far harsher summons. He looked up at Edmund, his features thoughtful. He wondered what he was thinking. Just as he was about to ask him what it was he was thinking about, there was a loud single knock at the door, its force sending the key falling from its lock, the piece of iron clanging on the wooden floor.

Both Dean and Edmund started at the blow, their eyes drawn towards the door. They wondered who stood on the other side. They were worried it could be guards to take Dean away, the council changing their minds. Edmund slowly turned the handle, not fully daring to open it. But when he did a crack he saw nothing but the young beautiful face of Clarice, her large smile beaming out at them. Her green eyes seem to sparkle with an inner cheekiness. Edmund dropped one arm and moved it in an elegant manner, bidding her entrance. She smiled warmer, walked in and stood on the key that had fallen from the lock. It's hard form hurting her foot causing her to yelp in pain and jump. She lost her balance and fell onto the bed face first. Quickly standing and brushing herself off trying to hold back her embarrassment to the stifled laughter of both Dean and Edmund.

"Well that was elegant," Edmund teased.

"Yeah if you were tired you should have just said love," Dean added.

"Shut up you two. You're as bad as my brother for tormenting me," giving Dean who was the closest a playful slap on the shoulder.

Dean feigned pain, grabbing a hold of his shoulder. He gripped it tight as though she had hurt him, his features turning serious. She just stared at him with narrowed eyes till he let his hand drop from his "wounded" shoulder. He smiled at her almost apologetically as she glared at him.

"I was just coming up to see where you were last night. We were meeting for drinks remember," she inquired.

"Yes I know, we were just so tired after the long drive up here we just crashed out," Dean answered rather too quickly.

Clarice looked round the room, sniffing slightly the scent of male sexual hormones overpowering anything else in the room. She looked at the messed up bedclothes, the fact that Dean had not got out from under the covers. It was obvious he was naked and equally obvious that not a lot of sleeping had taken place here.

"It's a nice room; I think you got one of the best in the hotel. Very "Romantic" I think," she said her eyebrows rising, over emphasising the word romantic.

Dean smiled shyly as he realised she knew what had happened the night before. Edmund coughed at the door, now they were the ones who were embarrassed, smiling to herself triumphantly as she turned the tables on them both.

"You know you shouldn't mess around with the Klymsky twins, we aren't to be trifled with," she smiled at the double edge meaning.

Edmunds eyes widened as he heard the name. Andre' and Clarice were the children of a council member, he couldn't believe their luck. Could they be used to put in a good word he found himself wondering? But he couldn't use them in that way. It wasn't fair and it certainly wasn't right. He also knew his lover would never allow it. Dean would face the council with no help from him or the twins. It just had to be that way; he had to face up to what he has done so he can then put it behind him.

"So are you going to meet us for a drink then later?" Clarice enquired.

"Erm well there's something we need to do first...........we........," Edmund started.

"We..........I mean I need to go and see the council," Dean finished.

"Oh right. Erm what about may I ask?" her eyes showed a genuine curiosity.

"I don't think we should be tel..............." Edmund started to say before Dean lifted a hand to stop him.

"I have told you, I need to accept what I have done," Dean said before turning towards Clarice," I killed two men, two humans, endangering the whole of our kind, do you think differently of me now?"

Clarice took a step back, not in horror or anger but just complete shock. To look at Dean, his soft emotional eyes, his warm young naive smile. He didn't seem capable of hurting anyone or anything, never mind killing two people. She was usually a good judge of a person's character, she was sure she hadn't got him wrong. No something about Dean touched at her heart the moment he smiled at her. It wasn't a polite smile, it was genuine. He had meant the emotion that was behind it. So for him to have killed two humans it must have been under extreme circumstances. She would have to talk to her brother about this; maybe they could have a word with their mother on Dean's behalf. Her thoughts were drawn back towards Dean as he watched her features for any sign off horror. She smiled at him, warm but there was a sincere sorrow in the gesture too.

"Dean I'm a good judge of a person's character, and I know that you must have done it for some reason. Whether that reason was just I don't know. But I know that you believed it was," she said finally.

Dean just smiled at her, Edmund rose his eyebrows thinking. Dean had clearly left an impression upon Clarice and even after hearing of his horrid past she still stood by him. He was like a demagogue, able to sway the thoughts of men's minds with only words. But was it more than that, it wasn't the words he had spoken that made Edmund love him. It was his eyes, the softness of his smile. It wasn't the words that swayed people it was just him, he was instantly likeable and seemingly incorruptible. Even though he did things they didn't or couldn't agree with they could at least understand why he did them. When he killed those two men Edmund knew it was out of Dean's control. He was maddened with pain, loss and grief, perfectly understandable from a werewolf's point of view as they were a species driven by their emotions. But whether the council would take this into account was another matter. And that worried Edmund. If not then Dean was in a lot of trouble and there was little that Edmund could do to help him. And that time was approaching fast. The clock beside their bed showed it was almost one pm. In two hours he would be freed, banished, or imprisoned. He was just glad they no longer used execution as a punishment.

Edmund tapped Dean lightly on the shoulder, motioning towards the clock. When Dean saw what the time was his breath caught in his throat and a small groan escaped his lips. He was scared to face them and that time was drawing closer with each passing minute. His future was to be decided by people who didn't know him, never even met him. But a single glance at the man opposite shook all those thoughts and fears from his mind. He loved him so deeply, so had decided he would face that council with a clear conscience and a pure heart. Both Edmund and Clarice saw the change that came over him, his back straightened, his chest puffed out in defiance and his eyes flashed with an undying determination. He had done nothing wrong. Not given the situation, so he had nothing to fear from them. Dean stood holding the covers as he did so, the quilt barely covering his modesty. He straightened his back and nodded at Edmund. He smiled warmly at Clarice as Edmund asked her to leave. After she had left the room Dean very quickly got dressed and ran his fingers through his hair.

Chapter 16

Later as the clock drew close to three pm they left their room, walking down stairs with a determination that clearly wasn't lost on the old inn keeper as he eyed them from the reception desk. They were both greeted by the bright warm early afternoon sun, its rays lighting up Dean's eyes till they almost glowed. Looking at Edmund and giving him a slight nod telling him he was ready they set off. Heading towards a large stone building totally out of character with the rest of the town, it was imposing, obviously far older and grander than the others. The gardens in front of the place softened the foreboding building only slightly, though they were beautiful and well maintained. But did little to distract from the sheer malice the place seemed to release upon its viewer. It looked like an old medieval keep. The dark windows and large staircase just added to the building intimidation. The grand steps were hewn out of ancient stone worn smooth by centuries of his kind treading them to face a fate Dean couldn't begin to understand. A cold and unbidden shiver ran down Deans back, he shook it away steely determination still in his eye. Dean led the way as they climbed towards the heavy wooden doors. Its surface now engraved and chased in gold, but this was a far more recent adornment. They were originally made to cause fear and desperation within anyone who had to climb these steps. But it wouldn't have worked with Dean now; his heart was burning at the prospect of losing Edmund.

The doors swung open as they approached, pushed by a pair of young male werewolves. They were greeted by a friendly looking man in a crimson suit; he bowed slightly and asked them to follow him to the waiting area. As they traversed the corridors Dean glanced at the walls adorned with ancient pictures and portraits of council members long since dead. The sheer weight of history seemed to strip him of his new found confidence, but one glance at the man to his left lifted his spirits and strengthened his resolve. He simply would not lose Edmund now. He couldn't he was all that truly mattered in his life. He was his life.

Their young guide passed beneath an arch hewn into stone and stopped, motioning for Dean and Edmund to sit and await their summons. Edmund sat as the man retreated out of the room, bowing again. However Dean was too worked up to sit down, instead he paced up and down in front of the doors that led into the council chamber itself. He was eager to get this over with, the sooner it was done the sooner he could get on with his own life, his life with Edmund. As to whether the council would allow him to do that was irrelevant, the simple fact was he was going to do it. He wouldn't be separated from him now. As he walked around the room he saw ancient stone reliefs, carved into the very walls. Seeming to depict the history of the werewolf race, Dean could see that his kind was once feudal in state. Split into clans each led over by an alpha, fighting wars for territory and members. Then something happened, one alpha formed a council to rule over his clan so the power was no longer held by one person who could use it to their own ends. This was the starting's of a democratic society that the other clans eventually adopted, over time the clans merged to form the nation that still thrives today. It was forbidden to defy a council's ruling; their word was law for they kept a werewolf's natural cravings for power in check. Without them they would eventually be driven again into factions, which wouldn't bode well for them. Dean was shook from his musings when he heard the doors creak as they were slowly pulled open, pulled by two werewolves in the same attire as the man that led them here. It must have been the dress for those who worked in the council halls.

The doors opened fully, their heavy weight knocking against the walls. Dean and Edmund were shown in by another man in a crimson suit; however this man was in no way friendly. His dark eyes held no emotion at all it seemed, not even a glint in their corner. His sour demeanour seemed to encompass his entire body, when he showed them to the centre of the circular room it was with a nod off head and point of clawed finger. Not a word passed his lips as he stared at Dean for an uncomfortable amount of time. His gaze soon shifted though Dean could do nothing but shiver at the way he had look at him. He felt almost violated by the stare, but he had to remain strong. It seemed like a tactic to unnerve and break down his resolve. The man took up a heavy and ornately carved staff, it must have been centuries old and though through all that time it had been lovingly maintained. Its gilt finials and engravings still as bright as they would have been when it was first made. Only at the floor end did it truly show its age, for it was worn and split after many centuries being placed on the floor with force. It looked like some sort of walking cane, but Dean had never seen one so ornate. Then without any cause the man struck the floor with the staff, its heavy fall resounding off the stone floor. Sending a loud knocking through the room, being echoed by the vast space, he repeated this manoeuvre another four times. With equal time in between, like the strike of a clock but it was little after three not five.

"Behold the council members of the western werewolf nation," intoned the man, as though he had spoken those words all his life.

A door opened on the mezzanine level, overlooking where Dean and Edmund stood, obviously for the council members to look down upon the accused. From the darkness strode a man, who appeared middle age though as a werewolf he could very well be older than Edmund. His thin dark almost malevolent eyes clashed with his thick lips curled up in a mostly pleasant smile, it was wide enough to reveal his impressive canines. His stride was powerful yet with a refined air about it. He never looked at neither Dean nor Edmund till he found his seat; his was the furthest to their left. Though he didn't sit, just stood behind his chair, he stared at Dean, but in an almost passive way.

"Welcome Council member Randon," the man intoned again, to the nod of Randon.

Once again the shadows of the doorway shifted as another council member emerged. This was a brute of a man; his broad shoulders must have been one and half the width of Edmunds. His muscles bulged in an almost grotesque way, veins popping from the surface of the skin. His eyes were small and seemingly cruel in nature, he eyed Dean without trying to be furtive. Dean merely stared back, uncaring of the protocol of proceedings. This seemed to give the man a little amusement for one corner of his mouth curled up into a snarl of a smile. He again stood behind his chair, staring at both men.

"Welcome Council member Dulane," the man said, Dulane gave the man a small nod.

A seemingly young man stepped out the door next, his robe like coat flowing around him as he walked towards his seat. He looked at Dean and cast him a pleasant smile, his eyes twinkling from the true emotion he had given. His face was thin in the extreme, his features definitely aquiline, long, thin and noble. He stood behind his chair and crossed his hands before him, the long thin clawed fingers grasping each other. He still had that smile on his face, when Dulane gave him a disapproving look however it slowly faded. He gave Dean a little wink which made him feel better. He didn't seem to treat the couple with contempt like Dulane or without care like Randon.

"Welcome Council member Aloysius," the man's voice the only constant in the room.

Then from the dark doorway came a flick of long black hair, it shimmered in the sunlight that shone through the high windows. Out walked a woman of such beauty that all eyes were immediately drawn to her. Her raven black hair hung down to her waist, interwoven with jewels and precious metals. Her corseted dress hugged her near perfect figure, the long flowing skirt dragging on the ground behind her. As she walked she looked down at Dean and Edmund, she smiled and nodded her head towards them. With great poise and grace she took her place behind her chair awaiting the last member to be sworn in.

"Welcome Council member Aliciana," he nodded towards her as she nodded back.

Heavy steps could be heard, as of someone striding with intent and purpose. A figure burst from the open doorway, his narrowed seemingly hate filled eyes stared at Dean, his gaze shifting towards Edmund, the hate never leaving them. A cruel, malevolent smirk crossed his face. Dean could feel the contempt the man felt for them both, it was written across his features like a mask. He stood behind the middle chair, his arms crossed over his chest. Never letting his eyes leave them nor his smirk leaving his own face.

"Welcome Council head Luken. This council is now in attendance, proceedings may begin," The man said, once more banging the haft of his staff on the floor to begin the hearing.

With this all the council members took their seats, each one of them looking down on the two men. It was a tactic to scare them and make them cower before the elders. It would have worked had Dean not been of one singular intent, the intention to keep Edmund. He puffed out his chest and met each one of their stares unflinchingly; he would show them he wasn't afraid of them. Then his eyes met the gaze of Luken, it was the nothing but the purest hate that lay behind those eyes. Dean knew from that moment he was never going to convince this man to be lenient. Luken took up a bunch of papers that were laid out before him, leafing through them with deliberate slowness. Dean huffed and shook his head to be greeted by the narrowed gazes of a number of the council members. It was clear that Dean was beginning to become agitated, which was Luken's plan. Seeing the other man smirk, clearly enjoying it Dean decided not to play along. After he had read through the pages of the report he put the papers down and stared at Dean. His eyes narrowed as he stared towards him.

"You have been brought here due to an incident that occurred a number of years ago, you reportedly killed two humans," Luken said.

"Yes, this is a very grave matter gentlemen. The punishment is a simple matter of exile," said Aloysius, "unless of course you can give us good enough reason for this infringement."

They all eyed Dean carefully, watching for any sort of reaction from him. But he was like stone, not even his eyes showed anything. Luken sat back into his chair, seemingly happy with the current situation. Motioning to the man stood next to Dean who stepped forwards.

"You may now speak, please give a true account of the situation as you saw it," he said, speaking directly towards Dean.

Dean stood forward, he had his head high. He put his hands behind his back and looked each of the council members in the eye. He relayed exactly what had happened to the council in the exact way he had told Edmund. He included about how he had lost all he had known after being bitten by a full werewolf. And how he was then taken in by Alexius, the name caused a number of the council members to gasp. A few exchanged worried and perplexed glances, Luken's eyes were wide with shock. Edmund and Dean both traded confused looks at their reaction. But the speaker who still stood beside Dean smirked, the smile quickly dropping as Dean caught it.

He had no idea why his old friends name caused such a reaction.

"This hearing must continue, you shall proceed with your testimony," said Aliciana, speaking for the still dumbstruck Luken.

Dean carried on with his testimony, telling them everything that happened. About how he crept into town, knowing full well what might happen. About how he attacked the man, and scared the other two. And how later that night they were hunted, and when Alexius was shot dead he went into a grief fuelled rage, killing the men with a ferocious intent. He finished his account with the killing of the police officer and the hunter. He had his head low at this point clearly utterly ashamed of what he had done He told them how he understood why he had done such a horrifying act; however he still couldn't be excused. His voice filled with a noble and honourable tone. As he finished he could see the council members take in what they had heard. Some nodded thinking, others looked horrified. But one, just one had a smile on his face. Luken was happy. They looked at each other, Luken and Aliciana leaning discussing something in hushed tones. Too quiet even for a werewolf to hear from any sort of distance.

Luken stood "we shall take a short recess to discuss this case; you shall be called back here within a few hours. Until that time you are not permitted to leave the town. A runner shall inform you when our decision has been made," with this he turned and left, followed by the other council members. Dulane was last, casting Dean a strangely remorseful look.

The man stood next to Dean motioned for them to follow him. Leading them out through the door, there they were met by the same man who had led them to the council chambers. His smile seemed not to have shifted and he bowed in greeting before leading them to the great door they first entered. Once again they were outside, welcomed by the scent of the surrounding forest and the brightness of the sunlight. Dean walked down the steps wearily; Edmund put his arm round him pulling him closer. He was exhausted, not from exertion but from worry. They both trudged towards the Wolfen Arms. As they walked in they saw a world of colour that was in complete contrast to the grey wooden sea that lay outside in the street. Red and blue lights hung in places, casting an ethereal purple where their rays met. The tables were old wood with chairs covered in black leather, at one such table were sat Andre' and Clarice both reacted to Dean and Edmunds appearance. They both looked terrible; the strain of being in the council chambers had obviously taken its toll on Dean who slumped in a vacant chair. He closed him eyes and asked Edmund to fetch him a drink, he felt like he was going to need it. Andre' and Clarice both sat down on either side of Dean, clearly worried.

Edmund walked to the bar, quickly ordering a couple of strong drinks before looking back towards Dean. He had his head in his hands, looking so very weary. Edmund collected the drinks that the barman had placed on the bar top. As he walked over Dean seemed to collect his composure slightly, leaning back in the chair. He looked up at Edmund with loving eyes as he was passed his drink. He had to keep it together; he couldn't show any weakness to the council. Taking a few tentative sips of his drink, finding it was to his liking. He smiled at both Andrew and Clarice who were still looking at him with concern etched on their faces. His smile grew warmer in an attempt to allay their worry. However it did little to ease them, Dean had to admit, keeping up the front all this time and the worry, plus the fact he hadn't slept for most of the night had taken its toll on him. But he would be ok, with all the things he had been through it had made a tough person. He would soon be in front of the council to hear their judgement and he needed to collect his thoughts before then. Slowly rising from his chair, he motioned from the others to remain where they were. He walked to the nearby window lent on the sill and stared out, the sun was starting to set. It was a beautiful evening; he could feel a light breeze from an open window somewhere else in the bar, the sun turning a ruddy colour. Yes tonight was beautiful; Dean just hoped it would remain that way.

Chapter 17

As he watched the light diminish through the thick glass of the windows, he quickly glanced at the clock on the wall, impatience setting in. The darkening sky mirrored his darkening mood. He was glad that Edmund, Andre' and Clarice had left him to his thoughts. Feeling totally exhausted after their return from the council chambers, he couldn't deal with questions. It wasn't their scrutiny, it was the relief he felt. All his worry had been vented all at once. After keeping his emotion in check he found himself suddenly devoid of energy. But he was slowly regaining his strength as he watched the last rays of the sun dying behind the forest, its deep ruddy tones extinguishing into the twilight, but its light still warming the skin of his face, as though even the sun believed in his cause.

Dean was absorbed in his own thoughts, but Edmund saw that his back was straightening and his confidence slowly returning. He was right to leave him alone to gather his thoughts. All three of them cast Dean an approving look as he stood in the window, his frame silhouetted against the deep red of the dying sun. He turned to them, with a warm and confident smile upon his face. His eyes sparkled, their blue hue seeming to become even more luminous in the deepening darkness of the tavern. Edmund assumed it must have been a trick of the light but as the barkeep turned on the bright main lights the glow didn't diminish. Edmund opened his mouth to say something when the door swung open, pushed a little too forcefully, the door clattering on the frame.

All eyes turned to the newcomer as he stepped into the bright lights of the tavern, the barkeeps face flashed with anger at the mistreatment of his establishment. But it soon mellowed as he saw who it was. His eyes were small but sharp, almost beady positioned too close to the hook of a nose. His lips pulled back revealing his elongated canines. He was dressed in a deep crimson suit with a black sash around his waist. Dean recognised him immediately. It was the crier from the council chambers; he looked exactly the same as he did earlier except he carried no staff. He walked into the tavern casting his eyes around the room with a malevolent intent. When he laid his gaze upon Dean he stopped, their lids narrowing. He strode over to him with strong and deliberate steps.

"Your presence is required in the council halls young one, you and your........... partner," it was with a strange respect that he

138

spoke. It shocked Dean because he always seemed to regard them with hatred.

Dean merely gave the man a small nod in way of gratitude and looked over to Edmund who was saying a quick bye to the twins. Dean gave them his own farewell, a warm smile and a quick pass of the hand. Clarice ran at Dean throwing her arms round his neck kissing him lightly on the cheek, a multitude of small tears streaming down her cheeks. But Dean's warm smile soon stopped her crying, while his thumb wiped away the tears that were still clinging to her cheeks. Kissing her on the forehead he turned to leave without a word being spoken between them. Clarice knew he intended to fight the council; he was never going to give up. Of that she was happy; Dean and Edmund really did deserve to be happy together for the rest of their immortal lives. She just wished she could help them in some way, but she couldn't think how.

As they were walking towards the council chamber Dean felt calmed by the waning moon. Its dim light cast elongated shadows upon the ground. He looked at his own shadow, it was long and strong, and strong enough to face the council a second time of that he was sure, looking over at Edmund, who looked a little worried. Dean knew he thought he was going to react the same way. But Dean knew he wouldn't, the emotional turmoil he had felt just tired him out. He started the climb of the steps that led to those huge iron bound doors that had given him such fear, but now it was with a solemn and quiet resolution. They were led quickly through the corridors till they once again stood before the doors of the council chambers. Their enigmatic guide quickly opened the doors; a harsh ruddy warm light met them with some force causing them to close their eyes against its glare. As their eyes grew accustomed to the brightness they could see the room was lit by bare iron torches, their flames licking at the walls behind them, leaving a dark layer off carbon on the stones.

Dean took a hold of Edmunds strong hand, interlocking their fingers together. Nothing would keep them apart, nothing on this world had that much power, and he even dared God himself to try. Edmund was his soul mate, he was his life and to take him away would be a fate worse than dying, for to be without him would be a living death. Edmund squeezed Dean's hand tightly, assuring him he was here. As they walked into the centre of the room the elders regarded them strangely, some looked at them with hatred others with sorrow. Aliciana herself couldn't even look at them; she had her eyes to the floor. Luken had a rather smug look, as he stared at the couple approaching. Dulane's look was the strangest, the first time it was with disgust he looked at Dean, but now it seemed more pity that anything else. The change startled Dean; he didn't think it possible for the man to show any positive emotion.

Dean and Edmunds grip grew tighter as they waited for the elders to speak; they remained silent for what felt like an age however. All the others were looking towards Luken, who no longer looked at Dean but through one of the many windows in the walls. The moon was getting quite high at this point, its silver bluish light washing over its amassed children. Then all off a sudden like he was broken from a trance he stared at the two men with a malicious glare, a sinister smirk crossing his face.

"Brothers, sisters we are brought here tonight to pass judgement over one of our own for a most terrible crime, murder," the way he said the last word was with a mixture of both disgust and triumph.

Dean was stricken dumbstruck by the word, he had never thought they would have seen it as such. The word made him feel sick, he didn't expect it.

"And as we have no facilities for keep prisoners, and we no longer execute our criminals there is only one possible punishment for such a horrible crime. EXILE! for the rest of your natural life," he almost shouted the last sentence as though it wasn't enough for him, but he wasn't allowed to pass a stronger judgement.

To Dean the judgement of exile felt remarkably light. He had lived in the human world for years so was quite used to it. Also Edmund seemed ready to settle down with him, so he was relieved.

"And furthermore, to decrease the possibility that this murderous trait can be passed onto any other of our kind, I wish to pass a motion to prevent him from having any further contact with ANY of our kind," Luken said his eyes lighting up with purest hatred and smirk off victory spreading across his face.

Dean couldn't believe it; he would be denied contact with any and all werewolves. That would mean Edmund too, he couldn't do that, and he couldn't live without Edmund. He could feel a small tear welling up in his eye, but the anger and hatred that was building up in his heart far outweighed it. He could feel the claws coming out of his fingertips, his canines extending. Aliciana stared at him intently. He was about to pounce at Luken when she stood up quickly and with much fuss, drawing his attention.

"Brothers, fellow members of this council we cannot bestow such a sentence upon these lovers so callously, they both deserve better. I suggest we allow them to spend another 24 hours together while we discuss the situation more fully. I ask of you all, don't be so monstrous," she spoke with a passionate conviction.

Dean could see some of the council falter, their gazes casting between Aliciana and Dean. However Luken still regarded the pair with as much if not more contempt. He also glared at Aliciana, he didn't seem happy about her speaking out of turn, standing briskly, his eyes brooding with hate.

"Sister, do we give privileged treatment to criminals now? Or should we punish them like we are supposed to?" he was clearly infuriated.

"That is not what I'm talking about, and you know it. I Just want to discuss this further we don't have enough information to pass such a sentence," she said in her defence.

"But we have discussed it Aliciana, and we have agreed upon this punishment." he glared at her.

"Very well Luken, however I ask that we at least allow them to spend another twenty four hours together, all in favour of this movement raise your hands," she said.

Aliciana, Randon and Aloysius all raised their hands to the amazement off Luken. He was out numbered, the motion was carried.

"Very well, the motion is carried. You will be allowed to remain together for another twenty four hours before the punishment is to be carried out," he was not happy about the turn of events but he had little choice in the matter, "You are dismissed."

The pair were quickly ushered out of the hall, the doors slamming closed behind them. The man who escorted them to the council halls earlier quickly slipped out of the door, closing it firmly behind him. Before he had closed it the sound of intense arguing drifted through from the room beyond. The man had a worried look upon his face, quickly wrapping himself up in some crimson robes, secreting his hands in his deep and flowing sleeves. He motioned for the pair to head towards the doors from which they entered. They headed down the halls at a hasty pace, quickly stepping out in the cold and bitter night. The man drew his robes closer about him, wrapping himself up tightly. Dean eyed him closely, thought etched upon his face. The man noticed his expression.

"I may be a werewolf young one, but I'm very old, even by werewolf standards. So I feel the cold," he explained.

"How old are you?" he enquired.

"Well I saw the Romans sack Carthage. So let's just say, I'm past my prime," he laughed.

Dean stopped dead, looking dumbstruck.

"Wait a minute! That was in 149BCE! Over 2000 years ago!" he was shocked.

"You've got a good head for history I see, I was only a child then mind. Not even bitten," he said thinking.

"But how can you be that old, you have to be the oldest werewolf in the world," Dean exclaimed.

"I'm one of the oldest this is true, but the true oldest werewolf to ever walk this earth is.............well dead," he looked saddened.

"I see. Did you know him?" he asked quietly.

"Oh yes I did, we all knew one another we ancients, we're a very rare breed child. Only pop up once in a while, under certain," he seemed to be searching for the right word, "circumstances."

"Which are?" he enquired.

"Oh that's not for me to say child, it is a secret kept by the ancients," he said apologetically

"I see, can I ask your name?"

"Of course, I'm called Octaviana. Now if you excuse me I wish to retire home. I bid thee both a goodnight," he said bowing slightly.

He walked off quickly into the night, the darkness shrouding him and concealing him. Dean stared after him for a long while after he disappeared; he was perplexed by what he had said. He felt a hand lay upon his shoulder, its heat warming his skin as well as his heart. Edmund was always there for him no matter what, that he knew deep in his soul. As he turned to face him, Edmund gasped and looked shocked. He couldn't seem to speak he was in such shock.

"What's up," Dean asked worried.

"Your eyes, they're………..they're glowing!" he said shocked.

"What, it must be the moonlight or something," Dean waved the remark away dismissively.

"No I swear they are glowing, they're bright blue. LOOK," Edmund said, dragging him towards one of the windows.

As Dean glanced into the window he saw his reflection and Edmund was right his eyes were glowing a bright blue. He blinked his eyes hard a few times trying to clear them, but the glow didn't go, it didn't even fade. Confusion set in, he couldn't understand what was happening to him. But he felt whatever it was, wasn't finished yet. He resolved to ask someone about it later. Right now he had to get his mind around the fact this would be the last night he will ever see Edmund. How could he live without him, he loved him so much. He spun round, tears emerging from his eyes and buried his head in Edmunds shoulder. Edmund wrapped his arms around Dean protectively, pulling him closer. The lovers remained in each other's arms, the light of the moon high in the sky washing over them, casting a spotlight upon their forlorn sorrow.

Chapter 18

The pair trudged back to the inn, their sombre mood growing darker every moment. As they walked in the inn door Andre' and Clarice must have seen their forlorn expressions because they both came rushing over with saddened looks upon their faces. But a look from both Edmund and Dean showed they weren't in the mood for talking right now. Instead they carried on walking to the stairs, ignoring all the other patrons of the inn. They stepped quickly up the stairs and headed for their room. They closed the door on that terrible night, and locked it out. Dean slumped onto the bed, his emotions weighing him down. When he looked at Edmund it was through a haze of tears, how could he possibly leave the man he loved and to never see him again. He just couldn't do it.

As he began to cry Edmund sat down beside him, pulling him closer to him. Dean buried his head into Edmunds strong chest again as he sobbed, his body shaking, wracked with sorrow. But Edmund felt the same; he shed silent tears as he stroked Dean soft hair. They clung together in their sorrow and grief. Neither wanted to leave the other, they loved each other more than people understood. Deans hold grew tighter around Edmunds chest, his sobbing slowed.

"Edmund, I'm not going to leave you, no matter what the council says," he said quietly, his face still buried in Edmund chest.

"Dean, we can't defy a direct judgement from the council. Their word is law," he said, still stroking his hair.

Dean lifted his head, his jaw was set, eyes almost ablaze with anger glowing a bright blue. He stared directly into Edmunds eyes almost making him flinch with his gaze. He narrowed his eyes, looking more malevolent than Edmund had thought possible. Clearly determined Edmund would never be taken away from him.

"Edmund I have been alone for a very long time, until I finally found you. I will not leave you, not ever. I love you Edmund, and I will not lose you," he said with softness to his voice, counter balancing his terrible expression.

"But......................," Edmund started.

"No there are no buts Edmund, I will not let you go without a

146

fight," Dean wouldn't let him finish, "my heart is yours and to live without you would be worse than death."

Edmund felt a lump in his throat and he lost his voice, he couldn't speak. Dean had shocked him by his words; they came straight from his heart. Honest and powerful. He could feel his eyes brimming with tears; he had to admit leaving Dean would break his heart. He grabbed Dean in a passionate embrace, their bodies pressed together so tightly they could feel each other's hearts beat.

Dean began to kiss Edmunds bare neck gently causing Edmund to quietly moan in pleasure. If this was the last night they will see each other Dean was determined to make it a good one. He let his right hand linger on Edmunds cheek while letting his left wander down Edmunds clothed hard body, feeling the ripples of tightly corded werewolf muscles underneath the thin, meagre cotton shirt. He could feel the body react to his light sensual touch, muscles quivering and twitching. Dean could feel an uncontrollable and all consuming passion rising through his soul. It was his werewolf lust building as it always did, but this time it was stronger, stronger than he had ever felt it before. He pushed Edmund over onto his back, his chest raising slowly as he eyed Dean with squinted eyes and a mischievous grin. Dean got on all fours, stalking Edmund on the bed, his eyes flashing, his canines extending as he became more lustful. He then pounced on Edmund, his sharpened claws ripping away his partner's shirt turning it into tatters of fabric. Taking a hold of Edmunds jeans waistband he ripped them clean from his body, the thread giving to Dean's beast like rage. Dean eyed the erect member before him like an animal staring at its prey, his eyes taking on a predators lustre. He raked his claws down Edmunds hips, tearing the underwear and drawing a few droplets of blood from his skin. Edmund moaned with intense pleasure and slight pain from the scratches. The stretched material finally relinquished its grip as the last few threads snapped, releasing the trapped erection hidden beneath. The swollen organ sprang from his stomach with sudden force and bobbed slightly. Dean ran one sharp claw down its underside, gently scraping its skin causing Edmund to writhe and the penis to twitch. Small droplets of pre-ejaculate were being released and began to run down its length. Dean collected this fluid with one finger and lapped it up like a dog, the taste lighting a fire deep within him. He simply had to have Edmund right here right now. He

147

grabbed the others legs and hoisted his backside up, using his strength to hold him in that position. Dean unzipped his fly, his own erect penis forcing its way out ready for use. He placed the head between Edmunds buttocks, usually he would lubricate his partner in order to not cause any pain but this never crossed his mind. Dean pushed his entire length into Edmunds squirming body, which seemed longer than it had been previously. Inch after inch was being forced deeper into Edmunds inside, stroking his prostrate and also tearing the walls in places. It felt like he was growing more endowed even while he was inside him. But soon all rational thought left Edmunds mind, soon it was only pleasure that filled his brain. The most intense pleasure he has ever felt in an entire century mixed with sharp intense pain too. He was soon bucking wildly, his body squirming underneath Dean who was just thrusting like something possessed. Dean's moans grew deeper and lower in tone, becoming more growl like. Edmund glimpsed at his lover as his body was wracked with such pleasure his eyes began to fill with water. However through the haze of salty tears he could see Dean, who seemed broader and more muscular than before. But it was his eyes that shocked Edmund the most, they were glowing a bright iridescent blue. Soon Edmund had to clamp his eyes closed has his body began to fall from his control as the pleasure intensified within, building toward a ferocious orgasm that threatened to rob him of his mind. He reached up and pinched his nipple, intensifying the already brutal sensations. Tears streaked down his cheeks, a mix of pleasure and horror. He could no more stop them than he could stop his hoarse cries as his orgasm ripped through all semblances of control and dignity. His own seed was ejected from his penis with such force he could taste it on his lips and had to screw up an eye to stop it from getting to the soft orb. It coated his stomach and chest, and even after that it still leaked from the opening in a slow but constant dribble that began to flow into a sizable puddle on his lower body. Dean however was still thrusting away causing Edmunds cries to grow louder and hoarser as his throat was robbed off moisture. Sweat ran from his brow and dripped from his hair to join the other bodily fluids below. Sweat, semen and blood mingling together on both their lower bodies. Deans own orgasm was growing deep inside him, he could feel his loins stir as they readied themselves to release his testicles payload. His testicles slapping against Edmunds buttocks as Dean humped with total abandon for his or his lover's welfare. He leant forward a little to gain more penetration as he felt he was close to ejaculation spearing Edmund deeper than ever before as he came to the point of no return. Dean came in long, intense and powerful shots, ten in total filling Edmunds bruised and battered colon to the brim as well as sneaking into his intestines as Dean emptied more and more into him. It felt like his stomach was bloating and distending with the amount off semen that was inside him. Deans howled loudly and ferociously more wolf like than it should have been. He withdrew from Edmund whose gasp was loud and mixed with both pain and relief. This released the flood gates as semen flowed from Edmunds now widened hole causing a puddle to form on the bed sheets between Dean's legs, and to his horror also there was blood too coming from the hole. More than there should have been, this shocked Dean from his trance as he looked over at Edmund who was breathing slowly and deeply, dampness on his cheeks from where he was crying. What had Dean done, he had no idea what happened it was like he blacked out. When his mind began to fit everything together it became clear. He had hurt Edmund internally, probably ripped something. Dean looked over to him and though there was pleasure and fulfilment in his expression there was also horror and pain. Dean couldn't look at him, shame, guilt and horror washed over him. He ran from the bed and crouched in the corner facing the wall and began to sob which soon became a terrified wail of fear and anguish.

It took a while for the pain from Edmunds rectum to subside a bit, yes it had hurt him but he had worse. Also the werewolf gene would allow him to heal quickly. But for Dean, it was far more serious because he had lost control and hurt him. And he knew that Dean would not be able to forgive himself easily, he was slowly losing control of himself. He didn't understand it, and if he was honest he was slightly afraid of it. He knew Dean would never hurt him intentionally, unintentionally was clearly another matter. He had shown that if he lost control then he could hurt him, only ever so slightly this time. But what would happen if he totally lost control of himself, he could really hurt him. It was now hours after the incident. Dean had sobbed and wailed till he was exhausted, falling into a deep sleep in the corner. Edmund nursed his ravaged body, cleaning up the blood and semen from his own body. He checked his insides with a finger and found Dean had indeed torn the wall off his colon. Though it wasn't as bad as it had first appeared, he had much worse and it would be healed in a small matter of hours. He just didn't understand what was happening to his soul mate. He was worried about him. Edmund decided to have a chat with the ancient they met, cure he would know something. But he would have to wait till morning to see him, and that was a few hours off. He closed his eyes and tried to sleep, but he had a fitful few hours nothing more.

He was asleep when a heavy knock came to the door; it was with some urgency the person was knocking. Edmund threw the covers round his body and lifted himself from the bed slowly in case he wasn't totally healed yet. But when he felt no pain he knew he was fully healed down there. He opened the door a crack to see who it was, it was an aide. Dressed in a crimson and black suit, his expression conveyed the importance of the message he carried.

"I'm here to fetch Dean to council member Aliciana, she wishes a private audience with him," he said.

"Well you will have to wait till he's ready," Edmund said.

"This is a matter of great importance, he must come with me now before the council call him back to the chambers," the aide rushed out, keeping his tone low and quiet, "please tell him to hurry."

Edmund had no idea what this was about but he saw the expression of the aide and heard the tone in his voice. So he closed the door and rushed over to Dean who was still asleep on the floor in the corner. Edmund walked over to his prone body, his chest rising lowly and deeply. He slowly shook him with his foot, trying to stir him from his slumber. His eyes shot open, red from tears the drops leaving damp trails along his cheeks. He had been crying in his sleep, his mind wracked with guilt and grief. Edmund looked down on him with both sorrow and a deep seated feeling of worry. Worried about what was happening to him, happening to the one thing that truly mattered to him. His heart grew heavy as his lovers situation started to look bleaker.

"Dean you have to get ready, Aliciana wants to see you in private," he said quietly.

"Edmund, I'm sorry. I don't know................." started Dean.

"I know, you don't know what's happening to you," Edmund finished, "but don't think about it now you really need to go see Aliciana."

Dean rose from the floor with a painful grunt, his muscles cramped and joints aching. The floor wasn't a forgiving surface to fall to sleep on. He tidied himself up a little, not caring about his outward appearance for his inner self felt dirty and sullied. He had practically raped his soul mate. Something like that wouldn't just go away with a night's sleep. He went to kiss his lover goodbye on the cheek who accepted the exchange without even a flinch which surprised him. He was glad Edmund didn't hate him for what happened; they would have to talk about it after this meeting. However he wasn't in the mood to speak to someone who was taking everything he cared for away from him. He threw open the door, the aide jumping back in fright and surprise. Dean's expression must have said it all for the aide looked worried. He gave a slight nod of his head to indicate for him to lead. The aide seemed to be in a rush, his movements fast and full off caution. Instead of following the main street when they left the inn the aide took him down one of the backstreets.

"I'm sorry young sir, but we have to make sure nobody realises where you are going. Especially none of the council members." he said hurriedly noticing Dean's expression.

"Why not?" he asked.

"This is just what I was told sir, I can tell you no more for I don't know more. I'm sure my mistress will explain all when you meet with her," his tone turning quiet and secretive.

Dean decided to just leave it be, it was obvious the aide knew nothing of the reason only what he was told to do. They traversed the paths with ghosting speed, changing direction whenever they saw others in their path. Left, right and then back on themselves to turn down another street, Dean was soon totally and utterly lost in the unfamiliar town. He was starting to get frustrated by the meandering path he was being lead on; he was just about to say something when they came out of an alleyway to be face with a magnificent building. Its stone carved with symbols and signs Dean had never seen before, they were beautiful. Tall stained glass windows depicting wolves in different aspects of their lives, sleeping, hunting, mating it was all there. The large brass bound doors shone with a brilliance even gold would find difficult to live up to, obviously polished daily for centuries.

"This is the council's personal chambers young one, Aliciana awaits you there," he said in hushed tones meant for Dean's ears only.

Leading him across the street towards the doors, as they reached them they opened both men being greeted by a young female aide. She smiled a quick greeting towards Dean and stared at the other aide. He shook his head indicating they had not been seen and the relief on the woman's face was easily recognizable. She quickly ushered Dean inside while the man remained outside for a brief moment before he too ducked into the open doorway. They lead Dean upstairs all the while flashing furtive glances this way and that, clearly if anyone saw him it meant something bad. But he couldn't understand all the secrecy. Aliciana was a council member surely she had the right to speak to the accused alone. As they reached the second floor they suddenly became more relaxed, their shoulders visibly sagging as their tensed muscles released. He was finally led to a small but beautifully carved wooden door, filled with intricate lines of tracery within an inset panel. The aide laid her hand upon the ornate brass door knob before turning to Dean.

"My mistress awaits you in this room young sir, please be courteous and please for your sake listen to what she has to say," she said her tone turning serious.

She opened the door for Dean who stepped inside the lavishly decorated living quarters.

Chapter 19

Aliciana stood at the window as Dean walked in, her thin, lithe form framed by the newly risen eastern sun. She looked as much a council member here as she did bedecked in her ceremonial robes, a silent but commanding presence that radiated from her, almost tangible. Dean realised he should never underestimate her. She turned from the window, a slight breeze lifting her hair playing with its strands like an invisible lover. She smiled at Dean with true love and understanding, throwing him on the back foot. He hadn't expected it from a council member.

"Dean, please sit with me my dear," she offered a hand and gestured to the antique sofa and chairs.

Dean almost didn't take it as a sign of protest, but he decided to be bigger than that. Remembering Alexius' words, 'just because the world thinks we are monsters that is no need to act like one' he took her hand lightly. She grabbed it with the deftness off a mother taking a child's hand, lightly but with assurance she wouldn't let go, leading him to the large sofa, its thick blue upholstery spreading beneath their combined weight. The velvet warmed by the sun was comfortable and inviting as Dean sat back resting his aching body. Aliciana turned on the sofa a little so she could look at him. She wore a beautiful dress in a dark blue that contrasted with the sofa so sympathetically you would think they had been made together. Its cut was both modern but with traditional undertones running throughout it, the lighter blue sash that pulled it in at the waist the most obvious of these.

"Now I'm sure you have many questions, but first let me tell you that I'm sorry," she said with conviction, "what was done to you in the council chambers was wrong."

"Well if you thought it was wrong why didn't you stop it then," Dean asked with a building fire in his eyes.

Aliciana jumped up and marched to the open window once more, she didn't want to face Deans questioning. The reason wasn't arrogance but fear, afraid that she would become ashamed of herself should she tell someone else. But the truth was she was already ashamed.

"You see Dean, we hold positions within the council only so long as we do as Luken says," she spoke to the wind and the outside world.

"So lady council member answer me this one simple question," he said politely.

"Anything that is in my ability to answer Dean," she said.

"What is the point in having a council of elders if you do as one man says?" he asked with a barb to his voice.

"But..............." was all Aliciana could manage before Dean cut her off.

"There are no buts, you are so caught up in your own little worlds, your trappings of wealth and power you forgot why you were made a council member. To help people," his voice low and laced with venom.

She was about to defend herself when she stopped the well-rehearsed words forming in her mouth. Instead she gave out a gasp of air as she realised he was right. Luken didn't care for the people, only his position and power. She walked back over to the sofa and slumped down next to Dean. She was finally ready to be honest with him. He deserved more from her, but honesty was all she could give him right now. Her confession began with the fact she didn't agree with the punishment Luken had levelled against Dean and Edmund. Also she knew that Dean couldn't really be blamed for what had happened; it was his wolfen spirit reacting to all his emotions. It was a situation he wasn't fully in control of. She poured her heart out to Dean who sat and listened in silence, waiting for the part where it helped him. He didn't care about her anymore; she had gotten herself in this trouble by not standing up to nothing more than a bully. As she went on saying that two other council member agreed with her and they had had a very large argument that night when they had left he jumped from his seat, fire and rage alighting behind his eyes.

"Then you should have quashed the judgement!" he shouted at her letting the anger out that had been building.

"Dean, we couldn't just do that to Luken. He would become enraged," she said defending herself again.

"So instead of telling someone no, you are going to screw up my life. And here I'm wondering why people call us monsters. Now I know, because we fuck each other over!" he shouted her down, leaving even someone like Aliciana speechless by his bluntness.

Dean walked out of her office, practically pushing one of her aides over as he stormed down the corridor. Aliciana appeared at the open doorway, tears brimming at her eyes. He was right, about all of it. She had forgotten her place and what that meant, but worse than that she forgot the people. The people she was sworn to protect and serve. She didn't deserve her place on the council, she didn't deserve her apartments and she certainly didn't deserve Dean's trust nor his understanding and pity. She used to be the head of the council, the most powerful werewolf in the western world second only to the ancients. Calling in her personal aide she slammed the door shut. She had a lot of work to do before tonight and a lot to make up to Dean.

Meanwhile in the town Edmund was searching for the ancient they had spoken to earlier, it wasn't until he saw a man wearing a crimson and black suit he got a break in his search. It appeared that ancients prefer to spend their time in the forests, it being their natural habitat. The man he was looking for had a cabin on a ridge overlooking the town, so Edmund set out to find it and speak to him. It was nearing noon by the time Edmund found the cabin, it was secluded like the man had told him, surrounded with trees on all sides, with just a foot worn path leading to its plain door. As he stepped onto the porch the door opened to reveal the man he had been looking for smiling at him.

"Good day to you young lad, how can I help you? Care for some tea?" he asked, to which Edmund nodded in surprise.

Showing Edmund into his cabin, it was sparsely decorated. A few ornaments and rugs but nothing of any expense. The thing that truly puzzled him was how friendly the man had become. He heard clanging and bangs with a quick apology shortly after.

"Not used to entertaining you see, couldn't remember where I put the other blasted cups," he laughed through the door.

After a few seconds of running water and sound of metal on metal the man came out. He smiled at Edmund as he opened the door letting in a slight breeze, with it a smattering of spring scents, perfumed flowers, heady fir sap and damp soil. He sat opposite his guest and crossed his legs.

"So lad, what can I do you for?" he asked.

"Wait hold on. How did you know I was there?" he asked the man who answered with a simple tap of his nose.

"You smelt me? From where?" Edmund asked shocked.

"Oh, well about when you passed the small lake a bit back," he said with twinkle in his eye, "not as young as I once was you see, nose isn't as hot as it used to be."

"That's almost a mile away, how could you smell me from that distance?" Edmund was enthralled.

"I'm an ancient lad, I can do a lot of things," he said with a wink, "now what brings you all the way up here, is it that lad your with?"

This gave Edmund a start; he hadn't even mentioned his name. How could he know such a thing? Edmund didn't know, but ancients could do many amazing things. He must have visibly jumped because when he stopped thinking he noticed how the man was looking at him. With a half-smile he grinned at Edmund, his eyes shifting colour.

"Started to change has he, yeah I knew it wouldn't be long. Not with all this strain he's under," the man said cryptically, "be hopes nobody makes him really angry or they might just regret it."

"What do you mean, he has been changing but I don't understand," he was worried more than ever.

157

"No you wouldn't lad, only another ancient knows what an ancient smells like," he said with sincerity in his eyes, "but there's no mistaking it, he's an ancient."

Edmund was shocked and dumbstruck; his lover was an ancient werewolf. Powerful beyond belief compared to even elder werewolves, he just couldn't believe it. He realised that was what happened, with all the stress and strain he been under it changed him physically. Explaining why his form was so different and also why he had hurt him. He needed to tell Dean this amazing news. Edmund rose from his chair in a hurry, eager to rush off to his lover. That was when the man called Octaviana moved; he flew from his chair and blocked the door faster than he thought possible. His eyes narrowed at Edmund, not menacingly but warningly.

"You mustn't tell the lad this, he isn't ready to hear it yet," he said simply.

"But he must know, this is huge," Edmund protested.

"NO! He cannot know till he is ready," he said more forcefully.

Edmund was about to protest further when he noticed the look in the old man's eye, he was warning him to not do this. It was clear that the old man didn't want any harm to come to Dean, and so he simply nodded his assent. If he was this serious about it he couldn't just ignore it. He slowed his rush down to a mere trudge, all the amazement of his discovery turning to disappointment and worry. Edmund pushed past the man's frail form, as he did so he felt the man's tightly corded muscles. Clearly this man could have stopped him easily. The walk to town became much harder than the walk up.

Chapter 20

Edmund headed towards the inn after his slow walk down from the forest when he bumped into Dean. He was striding back to the inn with purpose, his face filled with a rage he could barely contain. It was already early afternoon; they would soon be called in front of the council for the final time. Dean tried to muster a smile when he saw his lover, but he just couldn't hide his anger. He was infuriated by Aliciana not helping them when she knew they were innocent. He punched a wall in frustration; the loud crack that came when his fist came into contact with the wall was sickening. Edmund ran over expecting Dean to have broken his hand, but when he grew closer however he noticed there was a crack in one of the stones in the wall. He stared at the stone in astonishment, barely able believe the strength Dean possessed. Dean meanwhile looked over to Edmund in horror, clearly becoming terrified of himself.

"Edmund, what is happening to me," he asked throwing his arms round his strong chest.

Edmund was sorely tempted to tell him what was happening, but the ancients warning stayed his tongue. He closed his mouth and simply stroked his hand through Dean's soft hair. His murmurings calming his soul mate, he could feel his heart slow in his slim chest. The prospect of losing Dean brought him close to tears, he was petrified. Through blurred vision he could see a man approaching, his red and black visage easy to pick out in the grey background. Dean looked up and brushed his blonde hair out of his eyes clearing his view. It was one of the aides he had seen outside Aliciana's office, bounding towards them with all haste. It was obvious they no longer cared whether or not others saw them together. He scowled as the man drew closer.

"Sir, I'm sorry to interrupt but, my mistress has a message of much importance," his voice quiet and sensitive.

"It's ok," he said quickly, "what is it?" untangling himself from Edmunds embrace.

He seemed hesitant as he looked between the two, like he didn't want to have to be here. He closed his eyes before he said anything, composing himself and making sure he had the message right.

"My mistress wishes me to tell you this; she and the others will do what they can. However should things not go as planned there may be bloodshed," he blurted out.

Dean nodded his thanks as the aide backed away, smiling slightly before turning round and trotting away. It seemed getting mad with her had an effect on her. Whether it would help Dean would have to wait a little longer. The sun was rising higher in the sky; time was closing in on them. He knew they would soon be in that horrible place again, judged by their hard pitiless eyes. But it now seemed they had someone on their side, he felt a light touch on his cheek from behind him. He turned to see Edmund looking at him thoughtfully.

"I'm alright Edmund my love, I'm just scared because I don't know what is happening to me," he said feigning a smile.

"Are you sure?" he asked.

He nodded as he drew closer to his fated lover, pulling him into a hard passionate embrace, an embrace that could very well be their last. It was still a possibility they could lose each other. They could feel each other tense in their embrace as a nearby clock struck the hour, the hour of their judgement or their atonement. Dean buried his face into Edmunds familiar shoulder, this was it, and their time might be up. Shadows started to gather around them, as he lifted his head from his lovers hold he saw them, aides waiting to escort them to the council chambers. They smiled politely and nodded their heads in a show of respect, but all were as silent as death. Dean looked at his partner and hoped they would be together after this meeting, he also hoped his hope wasn't in vain. They took each other's hand and strode strongly towards the council chambers, determined and resolute. Aides walking by their side they climbed the steps, the doors opening seemingly by themselves as they always did. Inside stood their friends, Andre' and Clarice. Clarice was about to run towards Dean when her brother grabbed her arm to stop her. She wanted to say something, but as her mouth moved her voice seemed stuck in her throat. Even though he hadn't heard her, he knew what she wanted to say, simply 'good luck'. He smiled at them for their support and their concern. He didn't know what was going to happen, but he knew with friends like these and with someone like Edmund by him. He had the best help he could get. Clarice was about to turn away when she stopped and shouted out to Dean.

"Did you get our mothers message?"

Dean stopped mid stride, turning to face their friends with utter shock plain to see on his face. He could barely nod. Aliciana was their mother, he couldn't believe it. It was like destiny or fate had brought them together on the very first day they arrived. This seemed to embolden him, his chest puffing out, back straightening and his eyes growing harder. He gave them both a determined nod to which they smiled at his growing determination. He would fight, fight with all his might. Nothing and nobody would take Edmund away from him. Of this he was sure. The ancient they had spoken to earlier opened the chamber door for them, he was eyeing Dean strangely. Any other day this would have unnerved Dean, but this day nothing would deter him from his mission. He strode into the council chamber with Edmund by his side and locked the members with a steely gaze. They seemed to notice this, Aliciana and Randon flinching from his malevolent glare. He was through being nice, this time he was enraged by their lack of compassion and lack of courage to stand up for what they know is right. He stared each of them down, letting them feel the anger that was radiating from his whole body till he came to Luken. Though he blinked it was clear Luken wouldn't be swayed by a simple stare no matter how mad he was. So instead he backed down, letting his anger bubble just above the surface. He crossed his arms and waited for them to talk first.

"You two have been brought here this night because............." Luken began in a booming voice that seemed to fill the entire room.

"There is no need to bring this up again; they know why they are here brother. There is no need to open old wounds," Aliciana quickly cut Luken off.

"Sis................." he began again.

"NO brother, I want to hear their side," she said again cutting

162

him off.

She motioned for Dean to step forward, as he did so he could see Luken scowl at his approach. He was surprised by the way Aliciana had spoken Luken; it had appeared she was afraid of him when they were talking in her chambers. Seemed his rant had given the council member a much needed back bone. Smiling on the inside, his chances just went up a notch.

"Well there isn't much more I can add, apart from I am utterly ashamed of what I did," his voice carrying the weight of his emotion.

"We understand that Dean.............what we want to understand is what drove you to such a terrible act," explained Randon.

Dean looked into each of their eyes in turn, his heart and soul in turmoil at having to explain his past to these people. But it was the only thing that would save him, so he began. He told them about his childhood, being victimised at school till he grew up into a handsome young man. Then bullied about being gay and how his family was the only people he could fully trust. How he had lost his first love to werewolves. Lost his family to the fact he was a werewolf and then lost his mentor because he was selfish. He didn't even have time to think, just acting on total animal instinct, revenge being the strongest at that time. He didn't even stop to think before he launched at the police officer and hunter. And how he was terrified they were going to kill him too. He dropped his head in shame before the council. He felt such horror and disgust at his reaction towards those innocent men he couldn't look at the council members. He couldn't meet their stares, couldn't face their accusing faces. When he did finally lift his head his eyes were brimming with tears, collecting in the corners off his wide terrified orbs. But only Luken and Dulane were giving him accusing looks, the others however looked more pitiful than anything else. Aliciana looked towards Randon and Aloysius who nodded to her.

"So, losing your mate here would be yet another loss. After you have lost ever so much. How do you feel about losing him?" Aliciana asked tenderly.

"I can't lose him, he means everything to me. He is my life, taking him away from me would be worse than imprisonment or death," Dean answered his voice breaking slightly.

"And Edmund, do you feel the same?" Aloysius asked.

Edmund merely nodded at the council before breaking protocol and moving towards Dean, holding his hand tightly. Aloysius looked back to Aliciana and nodded to her. This silent exchange was confusing Dean but it was infuriating Luken. He threw his hands in the air and gave a frustrated rumble that reverberated in his chest. He'd had enough that much was clear, he shot an angered look towards Aliciana and stood up.

"Sister I fail to see what bearing this has to this hearing, but it matters not. We have already found him guilty," he said before turning on Dean, "we pass a judgement of exile upon you; you must not have any contact with another werewolf for as long as you may live."

Dean and Edmund was about to protest when Aliciana, Randon and Aloysius stood up, determined looks upon their faces. Aliciana motioned for the other two to sit back down.

"Luken, we disagree with the sentence. This young man doesn't deserve such a horrible fate for something that was out of his control," she said staring him down.

"Sister, I demand you explain yourself. How dare you undermine me?" Luken raged with barely controlled anger.

"It is simple brother, I spoke to Dean earlier. And though what he said hurt, it was the truth," she spoke with a quiet authority, "We have failed our people, by letting you run the council, and overpower us we have failed to do as we should."

Luken appeared to be shocked by her words; he didn't seem able to speak. He cast accusing looks at both Aloysius and Randon who didn't flinch but stood up and faced him down.

"I agree with our most honourable sister," spoke Randon.

"As do I," added Aloysius.

Lukens eyes grew wide as he realised he was slowly losing grip of his powerful position. He cast his gaze between the three before settling on Dean, his eyes narrowing in hatred.

"Furthermore," Aliciana added breaking Lukens gaze, "I find that Dean wasn't in full control of his actions so I rule that he is to be given a suspended sentence only. Who says aye?"

"Aye," said Aloysius.

"Aye," Randon added.

"But………." Luken started.

"No brother now it is my turn to speak. Also I call for a vote of no confidence in brother Lukens leadership of this council. Who will back me in ejecting our brother from our ranks?" she asked.

Luken looked winded, like he couldn't breathe. He was about to speak when all the other council members stood in support of Aliciana. Even Dulane who had been silent turned against his friend, just to keep his vaunted position. But his mind was still reeling from the sudden change in his fortune. He couldn't believe that he had just been given a suspended sentence. They had let him off. And now it seemed everything had backfired on Luken who was about to be ejected from the council. He was feeling quite happy with the turn of events and allowed himself to smile, that was a mistake.

Luken saw the smile on Dean's face and flew into a rage. He jumped down from the upper level and landed into a run, balling into Dean, knocking him over. It all happened so fast nobody had a chance to react in time. Dean landed on the floor hard, banging the back of his head, his vision swum for a few moments before clearing in time to see Luken going for his throat. His hands clamped around his neck and began to squeeze, cutting off his air supply. Edmund tried to pull Luken off Dean, but the elder was so much stronger. Through muffled hearing Dean thought he heard Aliciana shouting for the guards. He was slowly beginning to lose consciousness, the grip tightening. But something seemed to snap in Dean, his eyes shot open. Grabbing Luken by the forearm and squeezing tightly, when he did so he could feel a bone give way. Through the pain of his broken arm he released hold of Dean's neck. Once Dean could move more freely he grabbed him with the other arm and threw him with all his strength. Luken flew through the air and crashed into the wall above the mezzanines. Dean flipped backwards, dropping into a stooped stance. He bared his lengthened canines, claws extending from his fingers, his eyes glowing a bright blue narrowed in hatred. He growled loudly before he launched himself into the air and landed beside the shaken Luken. Gurgling on blood from his split lip as Dean grabbed him by his throat and lifted him from the ground. Luken tried to scrabble out of Deans grasp, with no effect as he continued to throttle him. He had tried to take Edmund away and then he tried to kill him, he deserved nothing but death at Deans hands. Throwing Luken again back down to the lower level, he landed on the flagged floor hard. Dean was in a rage, he couldn't control his anger. His roar was filled with nothing but the purest hate as his body began to change. He gained bulk and height, his legs forming another joint like that of a dog. Large black claws grew from his fingers and thick blonde fur began to grow from his body.

"He is maturing, nobody get in his way or he will likely kill you too!" shouted the ancient they had spoken to earlier.

His face formed a snout like that of a wolf, large slavering jaws filled with sharp and glinting teeth. Raising his head to the sky Dean emitted a piercing howl that caused all the werewolves present to shudder. He turned his bright blue glowing eyes towards Luken and stalked around the mezzanines. The other elders backed off out of his way, but he was totally ignoring them in any event. He had his eyes locked squarely upon his prey, Dean dropped to all fours as he got closer to pouncing. Then without warning he jumped into the air and landed atop of Luken, drool spooling from his fearsome jaws dripping onto the prostrate man's face. He seemed to savour his domination over Luken, but he had always treated him like excrement. Then he made the mistake of trying to take his mate from him, the final straw was when he attacked Dean. He deserved to know his place before he died. Dean grew closer to Lukens face, growling deeply he clamped his jaws to his throat feeling his front canines scrape along one of his vertebrae. He pulled and ripped out his throat in a fountain of blood and gore that splattered itself over his face and furred body. Dripping with blood, with his victim gurgling his last breath behind him Dean collapsed and fell unconscious. His body began to change back to his normal human body, bare and naked his milky white skin seemed to glow in the deepening sun.

Chapter 21

Meanwhile the next day Dean lay in a hospital bed, his beloved watching over him. Edmund had fallen asleep in the chair, his breathing heavy as exhaustion finally forced him to break his vigil. The sun was just rising; dawn gave the sky a ruddy pink colouring. A hand lightly shook Edmund awake; he stirred slightly from his enforced slumber to see a nurse stood over him. He blinked the weariness out off his eyes as he slowly came round.

"Would you like a drink or something my dear, or something to eat," she asked sweetly, her eyes lighting up as she smiled.

"No thank you, I'm fine," he replied suppressing a yawn.

"Are you sure, he's ok you know," she said reassuringly, "it takes its toll on a body to change so dramatically and so quickly."

"Are you sure he's ok," he asked his voice wavering.

She nodded in response and laid a hand on Edmunds shoulder before retreating out of the room shutting the door lightly behind her. Edmund remained sat in his chair and watched Dean till he fell back to sleep reluctantly. It was many hours later when Dean finally awoke from his unconscious state, he was dazed at first but soon his memory started clearing. He could remember Luken attacking him and thinking he was going to die but after that it was nothing but a blank in his memory. He looked over to the man sat in the chair beside his bed; it was the man he loved, his Edmund. He reached over and stroked his bare forearm softly, waking him once again. When Edmund opened his eyes he smiled at his beloved. Within a second they were in each other's arms, in a loving, strong embrace. Edmund hopped onto the bed and snuggled up with his boyfriend, with his soul mate. They stayed with each other for a long time, in total silence. Neither wanting to break the moment they were in, and both wishing it could last forever. Finally though Edmund sat up in the hospital bed and put his arm round Dean.

"Are you alright?" he asked worried.

"Yes I'm fine, a bit light headed but nothing serious," he answered.

"Can you remember what happened to you yesterday?" Edmund asked.

"All I can remember was Luken attacking me, the rest isn't clear," Dean's brow wrinkling through thought.

"Oh I see, well what happened was.............." Edmund started before the door burst open.

It was the ancient from last night, he was breathing heavily and it was clear something worried him greatly. He motioned for Edmund to follow him. Edmund was confused but did what was asked off him telling Dean he would be straight back. As the door clicked closed the ancient rounded on Edmund with a furious look in his eyes.

"I told you he wasn't ready to know yet!" the man rasped.

"But..........." Edmund began.

"No there is no buts boy, he got into this mess because he lost control and killed somebody," pointing to Deans room, keeping his voice low, "and then I hear you about to tell him he did it again and became an ancient in the process. Are you trying to send him mad?"

"I never even gave it a thought," his voice portraying his shock.

"Don't say anything yet, he won't be able to understand it and definitely not cope with it," Octavian said, "now go to him, he will need you."

Edmund nodded his thanks to the old werewolf and returned to the room to be with his beloved. When asked what he wanted Edmund didn't answer he just told him it wasn't important, that only they were important now.

Once again Edmund embraced Dean, and laid upon the bed getting as close as they could. He could feel the warmth radiating from Deans body, the sun warming them both through the wide window. Dean turned to his beloved; he was elated that they were

170

going to be together now. He planted a kiss off such passion upon Edmunds un-expecting lips that his breath seemed stolen from his very lungs. His mind upon fire as synapses fired throughout his brain waking his primal sexual urges. He returned the kiss with much more passion, biting upon Dean's lower lip. When they broke from the kiss Dean had a devilish look in his eye and a sly smirk upon his face. Moving and rolling till he was atop Edmund he ripped away the hospital gown from his body, revealing his soft, milky and silky smooth skin. Staring into his eyes Dean slowly undid the buttons of Edmunds shirt to reveal his heavily muscled hairy chest. Running his hands over the ripples off his lover's chest Edmund moaned as his erection ached to be released from its confines. Dean felt the hardening bulge and ground upon it in a gyrating motion causing Edmund to moan louder as he was slowly stimulated. The rough denim rubbing over his swelling glans, pre-ejaculate being released lubricating his hardening member. Dean chuckled naughtily at Edmunds expression as he ground harder and faster. Just then with Dean grinding madly and Edmund moaning loudly the door opened. Dean turned his head to see a young female nurse standing in the door way, her mouth dropped open, eyes wide.

"Oh I see your feeling much better," she said absently as she backed out of the room slowly before shutting the door.

Dean looked at Edmund who just burst out in hysterical laughter at being caught fooling around in a hospital, on a hospital bed. Dean grinned at his beloved, his cheeks forming little dimples his teeth flashing in the sunlight. He cocked his head to one side, his eyes twinkling like bright blue sapphires. He raised his eyebrows as he once again started to grind into Edmunds crotch. Once his erection was threatening to break free from the material Dean stopped and spun round nimbly. Working swiftly he undid Edmunds jeans releasing its caged passion, once free he shuffled backwards till his tight pink anus was positioned in front of Edmunds face who took the invitation immediately, deftly running his tongue around the tight muscles, tasting Deans most intimate and sensitive areas. Dean whimpered at the attention as he began to lap away at Edmunds fully engorged erection, running his tongue along its length. Taking its whole girth into his mouth Dean expertly began to suck on it, giving its bulbous crown his full and undivided attention. Edmund meanwhile was sliding his tongue into the entrance of

Dean's rectum, slowly lubricating it with his saliva. Once it was slick enough he began to tease the edges with his finger, letting just the tip enter before pulling it out. Teasing Dean's tight puckered hole, then all in one go he pushed the whole digit in. A loud hoarse moan told him Dean didn't mind the roughness. So he searched out for the small mound of flesh inside his rectum, once his finger brushed it Dean squirmed. He had found his prostrate; he slowly began to stimulate the small organ. Stroking it in a come here motion, Deans moans growing louder and more high pitched. Once he was in a good rhythm he began to lick at Dean's perineum, lightly running the tip of his tongue from the base of his scrotum to where is finger was slowly working. Dean was still sucking on Edmunds penis, using his lips to work the foreskin while his tongue lashed out at his glans. His moans were muffled by the large organ in his mouth, but he knew he was close to an immense orgasm. Edmund teasing his prostate so perfectly then licking him down there would eventually prove too much for him. He concentrated upon giving Edmund a great orgasm too, he began to deep throat his hard cock. Fast and deep till his throat began to grow sore from the friction. Edmunds moans grew deeper and louder, he was very close to orgasm, so he started to move his finger faster and in more erratic directions. This proved simply too much for Dean to resist as his muscles tensed and his anus clamped down on Edmunds finger. Semen gushed from Deans erect penis in powerful shots that never seemed to end as the milky white liquid pooled on his lovers chest and stomach. Dean worked with furious intent on his beloved organ as his body rippled with sexual pleasure so immense he nearly collapsed. He felt Edmund grab a hand full off Dean's buttock and he knew he was there, Edmund squeezed the soft, fleshy orb moments before he shouted out loud as shot after hot steamy shot of semen erupted from his penis going to the back of Dean's throat who swallowed as much as he could. But he just couldn't contain all off it as it began to leak through his lips and run down Edmunds shaft to mingle in his black pubic hair. Now it was time for Dean to collapse on top of Edmund, his body sapped. With the very last remains off his energy he managed to turn round and get snuggled up to Edmund as he cleaned off his chest of Dean's seed. Once his broad chest was clean, Dean laid his head upon it and listened to the strong beat of Edmunds heart till he was drifting to sleep.

Deans last thought before he dropped off to sleep was how

happy Alexius would be to see him so content.

This has been book 1 in the Kingdom of the Wolf saga

Story continues in book 2

Children of the Moon Goddess

due for release spring 2013

Dean and Edmund are finally together and their life as a part of the werewolf community has begun. But Dean's past still haunts him, he has to put Alexius' death behind him.

The pair travel to the forest that held so much pain and horror for Dean, to finally say a heartfelt goodbye to his old mentor and friend. However mysterious happenings throw Deans future into turmoil as he begins to sense a great change come over him. Once they return to Howling Falls they are soon whisked away by Octaviana and two shadowy men, they travel across half the world to meet with the council of ancients. There they confirm he is indeed one of their kind, a werewolf set apart from their weaker cousins. Far stronger, faster than the others and free from the passage of time. Whilst there he enjoys time with his beloved Edmund and learns of his species histories.

But fate has another destiny in store for young Dean...........
a destiny that could very well spell his end!!!

www.ingramcontent.com/pod-product-compliance
Lightning Source LLC
Chambersburg PA
CBHW060306290526
45789CB00001B/412